reat

ns,

i-

–

;

Rommel

The World Generals Series

"Palgrave Macmillan's World Generals Series will feature gr[...] leaders whose reputations have transcended their own natio[...] whose bold characters led to new forms of combat, whose determ[...] nation and courage gave shape to new dynasties and civilizations— men whose creativity and courage inspired multitudes. Beginning with illustrious World War II German Field Marshal Irwin Rom- mel, known as the Desert Fox, the series will shed new light on fa- mous warrior-leaders such as Napoleon, Frederick the Great, Alexander, Julius Caesar, and Genghis Khan, drawing out the many important leadership lessons that are still relevant to our lives today."

—General Wesley K. Clark (ret.)

This distinguished new series will feature the lives of eminent military leaders from around the world who changed history. Top military historians will write concise yet comprehensive biographies including the personal lives, battles, strategies and legacies of these great generals, with the aim to provide back- ground and insight into contemporary armies and wars as well as to provide lessons for the leaders of today.

Rommel by Charles Messenger

Alexander the Great by Bill Yenne

Montgomery by Trevor Royle

Rommel

Leadership Lessons
from the Desert Fox

Charles Messenger

palgrave
macmillan

First published in 2009 by PALGRAVE MACMILLAN® in the
US—a division of St. Martin's Press LLC, 175 Fifth Avenue, New
York, NY 10010.

Where this book is distributed in the UK, Europe and the rest of
the world, this is by Palgrave Macmillan, a division of Macmillan
Publishers Limited, registered in England, company number
785998, of Houndmills, Basingstoke, Hampshire RG21 6XS.

Palgrave Macmillan is the global academic imprint of the above
companies and has companies and representatives throughout the
world.

Palgrave® and Macmillan® are registered trademarks in the United
States, the United Kingdom, Europe and other countries.

ISBN: 978-0-230-60908-2

Library of Congress Cataloging-in-Publication Data is available
from the Library of Congress.

A catalogue record of the book is available from the British Library.

Design by Letra Libre, Inc.

First edition: June 2009
10 9 8 7 6 5 4 3 2 1
Printed in the United States of America.

Contents

The photosection appears between pages 112 and 113.

Foreword

NO FOREIGN GENERAL HAS EVER QUITE INSPIRED AS much passion, curiosity, and respect among Americans as German Field Marshal Erwin Rommel. His World War I experiences are the subject of serious study, his leadership in the Axis campaigns in North Africa was almost the stuff of legend, and his self-inflicted death by cyanide poisoning after a failed assassination plot against Hitler has been viewed as the essence of human tragedy. Decades after his death his son, then mayor of the German city of Stuttgart, received the utmost admiration and respect from the American forces and leaders stationed in Germany.

Charles Messenger's intense, fast-moving biography places Rommel's character, service, and lifetime of military achievements in perspective. But for all the demythologizing of his wartime record, Rommel's stature still casts an enormous shadow across contemporary military studies.

Born in 1891 into an average middle-class family in what is today southern Germany, Rommel showed an early aptitude for mathematics and an interest in the outdoors. Given the strong nationalist feelings of the time, it was probably natural to join the Army and become an officer—just like his father, who encouraged him to follow this path. As a young officer on the eve of World War I he strived for combat service, and he soon found it. Moving quickly through the ranks from platoon leader to commanding a battalion, he found himself in action against the French, and then later with the Germans and Austrians against first the Romanians and then the Italians.

Rommel proved quickly to be a charismatic and highly effective leader. He established a rapport with his troops, won their respect by sharing in their hardships, and was a diligent student of the new tactics and techniques brought about by the use of the machine gun and rapid-fire artillery in battle. By the later years of the war he proved himself to be an attack specialist, massing pinpoint fires, bypassing enemy strongpoints, and leading from the front to acquire the most up-to-date information and assessment. He was young, physically fit, daring, and lucky. By Christmas, 1917, he had won Prussia's highest decoration, the Pour Le Mérite.

It was these experiences that formed the basis for his professional teaching and his book, *Infantry Attacks,* written in the 1930s, which did much to shape German military training prior to World War II and even American military thought well into the 1990s. It was Rommel's combination of fire—massed and pinpointed to suppress and distract enemy forces—and daring maneuver to take advantage of the effects of that fire that provided the basis for much of the renaissance of American military thought in the post-Vietnam period. For at a time when much of the military experiences of both German and Allied officers had been based on surviving the risks and hardship of massed, trench warfare on the Western Front, Rommel taught the essence of maneuver.

Indeed, decades after historians commented about how much more effective World War II German units were, man-for-man, than most of their American adversaries, the American Army went back and seriously studied Rommel's lessons. And the principles of leading from the front, operating well-forward with a small command group, and personally directing the battle became ingrained in the American officer corps through repeated practice at the U.S. Army's National Training Center located in the high Mojave desert of southern California.

Had Rommel retired as a middle-aged former battalion commander in the 1930s, we might never have paid heed to his invaluable lessons. But, in fact, he did not retire; rather, through a combination of skill, personality, and self-promotion, he won the attention of Germany's new leader, Adolf Hitler. And, though he wasn't a member of the Prussian officer class and was no General Staff "insider," he managed through personal relationships to advance himself and win command positions of increased responsibility.

He missed out on the German Blitzkrieg into Poland in 1939, but he saw the effects. And with his profound personal experience and penetrating understanding of battle, his toughest task was to gain acceptance into the upper ranks of German commanders. His connections with Hitler did the trick; he received command of the soon-to-be-famous 7th Panzer Division and led it in the 1940 breakthrough into France. Here he quickly seized the advantage of the German Stuka in close air support, right in front of his lead elements, and pushed his men and the equipment to the breaking point. In his second war he again earned a solid reputation, and even public adulation, as an attack specialist.

Rewarded with a larger command in North Africa, he found himself in a difficult command environment working with the Italians and a long way from easy access to Hitler.

And it was here, where he made his greatest reputation as the feared "Desert Fox," that he also found the limits to his straight-ahead, forceful command style.

Hamstrung by limited logistic support, dealing with envious, mistrustful superiors, deprived of air superiority and usually lacking even close air support, Rommel proved himself again a daring lion on the attack, but, now in middle age, the arduous, punishing style impacted his health and personality. And, as many of us suspect, he also discovered that adversity in war is an altogether different test of leadership than pushing an offensive.

In North Africa, he succeeded in pushing the British forces almost to the Nile, and further burnishing his already fearsome public and professional reputation, but in the end his forces were made to retreat two thousand miles and his beloved Deutsches Afrika Korps was, ultimately, soundly defeated by the combined British and American forces in Tunisia in 1943.

In his last major duty, Rommel, now a Field Marshal, was second-in-command in the West, supervised the construction of Germany's "Atlantic Wall" along the English Channel and French coastlines, and was seriously injured in his staff car during the Normandy invasion. He was closely affiliated with the Nazi Party and, along with others of the *Wehrmacht*, took a personal oath to Hitler. Yet, subsequently, he was peripherally implicated in the plot against Hitler's life and, given the choice of trial or suicide, he spared his family the shame of a public trial by taking the cyanide.

Rommel's military reputation, though, has lived on, and still sets the standard for a style of daring, charismatic leadership to which most officers aspire, especially the up and coming leaders of his former adversaries.

—General Wesley K. Clark

Introduction

LIEUTENANT HEINZ WERNHER SCHMIDT, A VETERAN OF the 1939 Polish campaign, reported to Field Marshal Erwin Rommel's Deutsches Afrika Korps headquarters in Tripoli in early March 1941. His first impression of the man who was already twice a legend—as a leader in the elite Alpenkorps, or mountain troops, during World War I and commander of a panzer division in France during the 1940 campaign—was as follows:

> The General stands before me. His figure is compact and short. I gain a measure of confidence as I note that, although I am only of middle height, the General is shorter. He gives me a brief, powerful shake of the hand. Blue-grey eyes look steadily into nine. I notice that he has unusual humour-wrinkles slanting downward from the corners of his eyes to the outer edges of his cheek-bones. His mouth and chin are well-formed and strong, and reinforce my impression of an energetic, vital personality.

Schmidt had just come from Eritrea, and Rommel asked him about the situation there. When told that it was hopeless,

Rommel retorted: "What do you know about it, anyway, Herr Leutnant? We shall reach the Nile, make a right turn, and win back everything."[1] This was Rommel at his best: dynamic, positive, and absolutely clear and concise as to what he wanted to achieve. Schmidt also detected a degree of impatience. This was not a man who was prepared to stand idly by and wait for others. In a few days, however, he was to be on the move against the British forces in Cyrenaica, in eastern Libya, and have the action he craved.

It was, of course, in North Africa that Rommel really made his name. The cut and thrust of desert warfare provided the ideal environment to exercise his qualities of generalship. It made him a household name, not only in Germany, but among his opponents as well. Yet it has to be pointed out that, as far as the Germans were concerned, North Africa was a sideshow, a minor campaign compared to the Eastern Front, which would engage the bulk of the German army from June 1941 onward. That said, Rommel's command style in the desert illustrates how to conduct a rapidly moving battle, and its lessons resonate in the 1991 and 2003 Gulf Wars. By the same token his experiences in the mountains of Romania and northern Italy during World War I, during which he honed his skills as a combat soldier, provide lessons for the current conflict in the rugged terrain of Afghanistan.

He was also a charismatic leader of men. He believed in leading from the front, and instilled confidence in officers and the rank and file alike. Indeed, he would not expect his men to do anything that he could not do himself. But there is debate as to whether an officer leading from the front is necessarily the right way to conduct operations when in command of a division and higher formations. There is also no doubt that he pushed himself too hard, to the detriment of his health. This certainly happened during the 1942 campaign in Libya and Egypt.

Questions also arise about Rommel's relations with other commanders. There is evidence in his early career that he ignored his superiors' instructions, quite like Admiral Horatio Nelson turning a blind eye to the signals from the British fleet's flagship during the Battle of Copenhagen in 1801. Like Nelson, he had a much clearer idea of the situation because he was closer to it and was able to see opportunities that his superiors could not. This attitude caused irritation among other high-ranking German generals, and a view developed that he was an upstart who had no experience of the real war on the Eastern Front and was promoted to the highest rank simply because he was a Nazi toady. In North Africa he also experienced the problems of coalition warfare when dealing with his Italian ally. Diplomacy and tact were often needed to encourage the Italians to agree to his plans in much the same way as General Norman Schwarzkopf had to handle the disparate elements that made up the Allied coalition during the 1991 Gulf War.

The story of Rommel also reflects a major dilemma that has confronted soldiers throughout history. This occurs when it becomes apparent that the regime he serves is leading his country to disaster. Rommel, like all his fellow German commanders, swore an oath of loyalty to Hitler, an oath that no self-respecting German officer could break. It is true that Rommel became close to Hitler during the late 1930s, but by the middle of the war disillusion had set in over Hitler's conduct of the war. His predicament grew after the Allies landed in Normandy in June 1944 and defeat seemed certain. Should he join those who he knew were plotting to remove Hitler and bring the war to an end? Yet how could he desert his troops when they were engaged in a desperate struggle to prevent the

Allies from breaking out of Normandy? As it was, the attempt to assassinate Hitler the following month failed and eventually sealed Rommel's fate. Rommel's dilemma was similar to but greater than those faced more recently by U.S. forces in the conduct of the war in Iraq, especially in the revelations of torture and mistreatment of prisoners in Abu Ghraib jail in Baghdad and the policy of denying the inmates of Guantánamo any of the rights that a true democracy is proud to uphold.

Field Marshal Erwin Rommel is a character who has always fascinated and will certainly continue to do so. As we approach the seventieth anniversary of the beginning of World War II, it is fitting that we should take another look at this charismatic man and determine what we can learn for the future from his extraordinary career.

Charles Messenger
London, October 2008

CHAPTER 1

The Formative Years

THE MAN WHO WOULD BECOME GERMANY'S MOST
respected general, at least in the eyes of the Western Allies, was
born on November 12, 1891, in Heidenheim, near Ulm, in
the state of Württemberg in southern Germany. Erwin Rommel's father was a schoolteacher, and the family was of modest
means. Germany in the late nineteenth century had been
united as one country under the king of Prussia for twenty
years, although its states continued to enjoy varying degrees of
autonomy. On the international scene, Germany was a major
power, especially after it defeated France in 1870 and allied itself with the Austro-Hungarian Empire.

Erwin Rommel was an unremarkable boy and was not
considered academic, although he did in his teens develop a

deep interest in mathematics, a subject in which both his father and grandfather were able. He also became keen on outdoor pursuits, especially bicycling and skiing. Like many others of his generation he was enthusiastic about the idea of flight and seriously considered applying for a job at Count Ferdinand von Zeppelin's airship works at Friedrichshafen, on Lake Constance, within the Württemberg kingdom. His father, however, had other plans for him. Rommel Senior had been an artillery officer and urged his son to become a professional soldier.

By the time Rommel was seventeen and of military age, the generally accepted way of gaining a commission in the German army was to enlist as an officer candidate. He would then serve in the ranks and, if recommended by his officers, would attend an officer training school. Rommel wanted to follow his father and become an artilleryman, but this arm of the service was second only to the cavalry in terms of social prestige and the Rommel family lacked the connections necessary for entry. Erwin then tried the engineers, again without success, and so applied to the infantry. He was accepted by a local regiment, the 124th Infantry (6th Württemberg), and joined it in July 1910. Rommel soon impressed his superiors, and before the year was out, he had been promoted to sergeant. Furnished with the necessary recommendations, he entered the Royal War School at Danzig (today Gdansk in Poland) the following March. The course there lasted for eight months, and in January 1912 Lieutenant Erwin Rommel rejoined the 124th Infantry.

As war clouds gathered over Europe, Rommel worked hard to become a competent junior officer. His service included an attachment to the artillery in order to broaden his military education. He was still on detachment when war erupted in August 1914 but was posted back to his regiment, which was mobilized as an element of the German Fifth Army, one of seven earmarked for the invasion of France and Belgium. The plan was for the northern armies to advance through Belgium and Luxembourg. The right wing was then supposed to swing west of Paris so as to envelop it, outflanking the Allied armies.

The Fifth Army and its southern neighbor, the Sixth, were intended to remain on the defensive and be prepared to receive an expected French counterattack to regain Alsace and Lorraine, territories that had been lost to the Germans in 1870. The French duly attacked and were bloodily repulsed in what became known as the Battle of the Frontiers. Helmuth von Moltke, in overall command in the West, was persuaded to allow the Fifth and Sixth Armies to follow up this victory and take to the offensive. It meant, however, that he would now be unable to reinforce his right wing, which had the decisive role of enveloping Paris.

Rommel's regiment had spent the intervening time training near the border, during which he suffered an upset stomach. He blamed the greasy food and freshly baked bread that they had been eating, but it was to plague him on and off for the next few weeks. He would not allow his gastric discomfort to interfere with his duties, however. On August 18 the armies began their advance, crossing the border into Luxembourg. The next day Rommel heard guns fired in anger for the first time as his regiment passed close to the French fortress of Longwy. He then found himself largely involved in carrying out reconnaissances and as a bearer of messages, which left him very short of sleep. Finally, on August 22, Rommel saw his first combat when he led his platoon in an attack against the village of Bleid in the extreme southeastern corner of Belgium. It took place in fog, and his platoon was soon separated from the rest of the battalion. Undeterred, Rommel pressed on and captured the village. His personal courage and eagerness to seize the initiative were amply demonstrated. He knew what his mission was and had not allowed himself to be diverted from it even when he found himself on his own.

The 27th Division, of which Rommel's regiment formed a part, now crossed the River Meuse and began to press the French back westward. In further clashes Rommel gained a respect for the French artillery, especially the 75mm field gun with its very rapid rate of fire, and quickly recognized the importance of digging in every time his men came to a halt in close proximity to the enemy. In early September he was appointed battalion adjutant, making him his commanding officer's right-hand man. This post gave Rommel more scope to use his initiative. When not carrying out reconnaissances or acting as a liaison officer, he was usually to be found with the forward companies. Much of the fighting during the next few weeks was in the woods, and Rommel quickly learned how difficult command and control were in that environment. Indeed, it was during one of these fights, near Varennes, some fifteen miles northwest of Verdun, on September 24 that Rommel's luck finally ran out. He had taken command of two squads totaling some twenty men—the largest unit which he believed could be controlled in this type of fighting—and was attempting to press forward under heavy French fire. At one stage he found himself on his own with five Frenchmen facing him some twenty yards away. He fired his rifle and downed two of them, but then discovered that his magazine was empty. With no time to reload he charged the remainder, only to be struck by a bullet in the upper leg. He managed to roll behind an oak tree and, after a short time, his men succeeded in rescuing him.

Rommel was evacuated back to Germany and was informed that he had been awarded the Iron Cross Second

Class. He was discharged from the hospital, just before Christmas 1914, with his wound still not healed. He should have been posted to a replacement battalion, which was responsible for training recruits and looking after soldiers convalescing from wounds and sickness prior to being sent back to the front. This prospect did not appeal to Rommel, the man of action, and so January 1915 found him back with his regiment, now in the hilly and wooded Argonne region of France.

The conditions there were very different from the open warfare that Rommel had previously experienced. Both sides were now dug in, and the war had become static. Rommel was given command of a company in his old battalion, which delighted him. He later observed: "For a twenty-three-year-old officer there is no finer job than that of a company commander. Winning the men's confidence requires much of a commander. He must exercise care and caution, look after his men, live under the same hardships, and—above all—apply self-discipline. But once he has their confidence, his men will follow him through hell and high water."[1]

His first task was to improve the trenches, some of which were waterlogged, and to make the dugouts more secure against artillery fire, which was frequent. The impact of the French guns was even more significant since the German supporting artillery was suffering an ammunition shortage at the time. The opportunity for offensive action came on January 29, when the 27th Division was ordered to carry out a major raid on the French lines. Rommel led his company with great verve, but it got ahead of the other companies and found itself in danger of being cut off. It had to fight partway back, but the ground that had been captured did yield some benefit. The trenches that Rommel now occupied were higher than the original German front line and so were less waterlogged. For his conduct during this attack he was awarded the Iron Cross First Class.

The next three months saw Rommel's regiment inch its way closer to the French lines. There was a steady trickle of casualties, especially from French mortar fire. Rommel felt the loss of men under his command, especially those who had been badly wounded. In May 1915 a more senior lieutenant, who had no command experience, took over his company. The battalion commander wanted to post Rommel to another company, but he insisted on remaining with the men to whom he had grown so close. It must, however, have been difficult for the new company commander to have had such a highly decorated and combat-experienced officer under him, but Rommel gives no indication of any friction between them. Indeed, on June 30 the company was involved in an assault on the French sector that Rommel had attacked and then pulled back from in January. Rommel's platoon was the company reserve, but seeing that the assault platoons were faltering, he took charge and the attack was successful. Mindful that he had very nearly been cut off during the January attack, he resisted the temptation to press on too far and concentrated on consolidating with the units on his flanks so as to be able to successfully resist any French counter-attacks.

Rommel then found himself serving as deputy for other company commanders, who were absent because they were ill or on leave, and as such took part in another successful attack in early September. Rommel's company mounted an attack on an objective some two hundred yards inside the French lines. He attributed its success to careful preparation, including several rehearsals to ensure that his men were entirely clear about what was required of them.

His circumstances now changed dramatically. Later that month he was promoted to first lieutenant and posted away from the 124th Regiment. His new assignment was as a company commander in the Württemberg Mountain Battalion, which was being formed in Münsingen, a small town some thirty miles southeast of Stuttgart, to fight in the Vosges Mountains. His new commanding officer was, in Rommel's words, "a martinet."[2] Even so, although the men came from several different units, it was a happy battalion from the outset. The training was rigorous, but Rommel thrived on it. Even better, the battalion moved to Austria in early December 1915 for ski training. Arduous skiing all day was followed by sing-alongs in the evening, which helped to further bind the unit. The men were fed Austrian rations, which included wine and cigarettes and were clearly better than the German ration.

Everyone in the battalion expected that it would be sent to the Italian Front once it had completed its training. Italy had entered the war in May 1915 and was now fighting the Austrians in the mountainous Tirol, through which ran their mutual border. It seemed logical that this is where the Württembergers would be employed. But four days after Christmas the battalion found itself on a train headed for the Western Front. Its destination was the Vosges Mountains at the southeast end of the front, which had seen little fighting since the outbreak of war, thanks to the nature of the terrain, which strongly favored defense. The battalion occupied a 10,000-yard-long sector, and because it did not have the men to form a continuous defense, it relied on a series of strongpoints. The French front line was not close, and the sector remained quiet, which was in contrast to what Rommel had experienced in the Argonne. He did, however, conduct one successful raid at the beginning of October. The object was to capture prisoners so as to gain intelligence on the French opposite the Württembergers. Rommel made a very careful reconnaissance before drawing up his plan, then decided to make his point of attack midway between two French strongpoints. The assault group would enter the French trench and split, with half going left and the remainder right. Two other teams would cut the wire opposite each strongpoint to enable the assault group to get back to its own lines. Rommel, as usual, was with the assault group. The raid was brilliantly successful, catching the French by surprise and yielding eleven prisoners. There would be little time to celebrate, though, since the battalion was ordered elsewhere, to a new theater of war.

On August 27, 1916, Romania had entered the war on the Allied side. It had been encouraged by the German failure to capture Verdun and the Allied offensives then taking place on the Western, Eastern, and Italian Fronts, and hoped to be rewarded at war's end with territory in Austro-Hungarian Transylvania. It was a decision that Romania would quickly regret. It soon found itself under attack from German and Austrian troops in the west and Bulgarian forces in the south. Rommel's battalion was ordered to Romania in late October and placed under command of the Schmettow Cavalry Corps at the western end of the Transylvanian Alps, which guarded the northwestern approaches to Romania. He was to be faced with his toughest challenge yet.

The Württemberg Mountain Battalion was ordered to establish a position on a hill some 6,000 feet high. A Bavarian division had a few days earlier attempted to force its way through two key passes, Vulcan and Skurduk, but was beaten back. The battalion set off with each man carrying four days' rations and all his ammunition and equipment, but they lacked winter clothing. They encountered Bavarians who had become separated from their units and could tell them little of the situation. With nightfall came rain, but the Württembergers continued upward. Eventually, unable to go any farther on the steep and rocky ground, they halted. They tried to build a fire from wet pine branches, but it only gave off smoke and no heat. At daybreak they resumed the climb, crossing the snow line and eventually reaching the summit of Hill 1794, where there was little shelter. The captain in command recommended that they withdraw from the summit, and the battalion medical officer also warned that the conditions would quickly result in most men becoming incapacitated. The sector commander turned down the request, with the warning that any man who vacated the position would be liable to court-martial. They endured another twenty-four hours, by which time some 90 percent of the men were suffering from frostbite and other cold-related injuries. They were then relieved by troops who had the right equipment for coping with such a bleak situation. The Württembergers were now provided with the necessary equipment, including pack animals, and Rommel's company occupied another hill amid better weather. He had come through a bitter experience without faltering, demonstrating once again his physical and mental toughness.

Preparations were now well under way for a renewed offensive, and Rommel's battalion played its part in breaking through the Romanian defenses in the mountains. In one attack his company secured its objective, but no sooner had it done so than the Romanians counterattacked amid dense fog. One of his platoons, which had pressed too far forward, became isolated and had to fight its way back. Luckily, the sun then began to break through the fog, and Rommel was able to keep the Romanians at bay with rifle and machine-gun fire until the company was reinforced. Rommel's determination averted what might have been a disaster.

In late November 1916 Rommel returned to Germany on leave for a very special purpose. As a cadet at Danzig, Rommel had fallen in love with Lucie Mollin, the dark and beautiful daughter of a Prussian landowning family who was studying languages there. The attraction was mutual, and they were soon engaged, at least unofficially. As in many other armies of the day, the German army frowned on officers getting married too young. Rather, they were expected to concentrate on their profession. Now, with Rommel an experienced and proven combat officer, the marriage was finally able to take place. Lucie and he were to be the closest of companions for the remainder of Rommel's life. He drew great strength from her, and when they were apart he wrote to her frequently, often daily, sometimes voicing his innermost thoughts that he would not share with others.

Rommel's honeymoon was all too brief, and he was back in Romania by mid-December. Bucharest, the capital, had fallen. The Württemberg Mountain Battalion joined the Alpine Corps, which was tasked with clearing the mountains to the northeast of the city. Rommel, his company reinforced by a heavy-machine-gun platoon, was allowed plenty of freedom to use his own initiative. His emphasis on thorough reconnaissance paid dividends, enabling him to surprise groups of Romanians by attacking from an unexpected direction and to lay successful ambushes. He also employed bluff to persuade groups of Romanians to surrender. By the end of this phase of the campaign Rommel often commanded two companies, with supporting heavy weapons platoons. This concept of putting together ad hoc groups of infantry and machine guns to suit the requirements of a particular operation was now commonplace in the battalion. It was a forerunner of the *Kampfgruppen* (battle groups) that Rommel was to use so successfully in North Africa twenty-five years later.

Early in 1917 Rommel's battalion was withdrawn from Romania. It was destined for the Western Front, but spent some weeks in army reserve. Thereafter Rommel's command, which now consisted of two rifle companies and a machine-gun company, was placed in corps reserve. This enabled him to carry out some rigorous refresher training. This was clearly very effective and impressed the battalion commander to the extent that he arranged for every company in the battalion to rotate through what became, for all intents and purposes, Rommel's training school. Then it was back to the Vosges for a spell of trench duty on the Hilsen ridge.

Late July 1917 saw the battalion once more on the move. A week's journey by train took it back to Romania. Even though most of the country had been overrun, by the end of 1916 the Romanian army, with Russian support, was still fighting on. Indeed, in July 1917 Romanian forces had taken part in the final Russian offensive and enjoyed some initial success. When Rommel and his men arrived, an Austro-German counteroffensive was being prepared and they were deployed to much the same area that they had been in at the beginning of the year. The Württembergers were placed under the command of a Bavarian infantry brigade. Their task was to seize the dominant Mount Cosna, which held the key to the Ojtoz Pass, through which ran a route leading to the fertile plains of southern Romania. This time Rommel enjoyed his largest command yet—six rifle and three machine-gun companies, which represented almost the entire battalion. Information on the enemy was sparse, but his emphasis on reconnaissance once more paid off. He established that the Romanians had recently evacuated some of their forward positions and so he immediately occupied them. Another of his patrols then surprised a group of resting Romanians and brought them back, together with five machine guns. The main attack itself was supposed to take place in the afternoon of August 9, but rather than sacrifice the initial surprise that he had gained, Rommel immediately pushed upward with two companies and succeeded in penetrating the Romanian lines to a depth of 1,100 yards, although in the process he was wounded in the arm. The next day Rommel's men reached the summit of Mount Cosna after a tough fight.

The Romanians still held positions to the east and northeast of the mountain, however, and this meant that the Germans still could not get through the pass. In spite of his men's exhaustion Rommel now prepared to attack these positions, but instead he received orders to withdraw to the ridge from which he had launched his attack on the mountain. The Russians had managed to break through in the north and were now threatening the German left flank. Then, on August 13, the Romanians launched an attack. The Württembergers hung on desperately, their casualties mounting. Luckily, the following morning reinforcements arrived and the crisis passed. Six days later Rommel led a second and successful assault on the summit of Mount Cosna. After repulsing a counterattack the battalion was withdrawn into reserve.

Once more Rommel had covered himself in glory. Yet the two weeks' fighting had cost his battalion some five hundred casualties, and he was in a bad way. His exertions, both physical and mental, had left him exhausted, and he was feverish. There was, too, his wounded arm. Not surprisingly, he was evacuated to Germany and went with his wife to recuperate on the Baltic coast. In early October he returned to his battalion. It had been resting and reorganizing in the southernmost Austrian state of Carinthia and was now preparing for battle once more, this time on the Italian Front.

For almost three and a half years the Italians had been battering their heads against the Alps through which their border with Austria ran. Their primary objective was the principal Austro-Hungarian port of Trieste at the head of the

Adriatic. Not until August 1917 did they make any significant progress, when, in what was called the eleventh battle of the Isonzo River, they managed to advance far enough to threaten Trieste. The Austrians asked for German help to shore up their defenses, and the German Fourteenth Army, of which the Alpine Corps formed part, was dispatched. The plan was to mount a counteroffensive designed to attack across the Isonzo and drive the Italians off the mountains to its west. The defenses were strong, consisting of a forward line on the river itself, a second line behind it, and a third line running through the mountains. The Alpine Corps was to secure this last line, with the Württemberg Mountain Battalion being responsible for dealing with certain identified artillery batteries and then securing the summit of Mount Matajur.

As so often had been the case, Rommel was given a number of companies—three rifle and one machine-gun. The attack opened on October 24 with a very accurate five and a half hours of bombardment that pulverized the Italian defenses. At 7:30 A.M. the assault troops went into action. Rommel's detachment was initially in support, but once the Italian first line was taken it became the battalion advance guard. It began to climb the slopes leading to the Italian second line. It was pouring rain, but at least the trees and thick undergrowth provided cover from the Italian positions above. While a Bavarian regiment on his left flank made a frontal assault, Rommel and his men moved obliquely, taking advantage of the cover to overrun isolated Italian positions, which they usually took from the rear. Rommel himself likened the operations to those around Mount Cosna in August.[3] Eventually they arrived below a strongly fortified hill on the ridge that represented the third line of Italian defenses. This line barred the way to Mount Matajur, which lay at the other end of the ridge. The

Bavarians were already on the ridge and in the saddle facing the hill, and their commander tried to put Rommel under his command. Rommel demurred, stating that this decision was a matter for his own commanding officer. By now dusk had arrived and he formulated a plan for bypassing the hill, leaving the Bavarians to deal with it. His battalion commander arrived at Rommel's command post at 5:00 the next morning, and just before dawn. He approved Rommel's plan, and Rommel set off.

Dropping down some 150 feet from the crest, albeit under Italian machine-gun fire that caused casualties, Rommel and his men reached a clump of bushes where he linked up with one of his other companies. In the meantime the Bavarians had begun their attack on Hill 1114, and the noise of battle did provide some cover as the Württembergers moved off westward, dropping a little farther away from the crest and taking advantage of the undergrowth. It was crucial that the Italians should not see them. His scouts then stumbled across an Italian heavy artillery position, which they seized without a shot being fired. Other prisoners were also taken. Once they moved some one and a half miles from Hill 1114 they turned uphill and successfully stormed the surprised Italian defenses. But now Rommel found himself in a dilemma. This part of the ridge was bare of vegetation, and facing him was another peak, Mount Kuk, but he lacked the strength in numbers to attack it. In the meantime his men were under fire and the Italians were threatening a counterattack. Leaving his lead company where it was, Rommel withdrew the remainder of his force to a saddle on the ridge, which provided some cover. The lead company was now embroiled in a close-quarters fight against superior numbers. The position was critical, but Rommel was equal to it. He quickly took his other company round to the flank and attacked the Italians. His lead company now also attacked. Totally surprised by this, the Italians, totaling over five hundred, surrendered.

With the crisis now passed, Rommel could get on with pressing toward Mount Matajur. A track that had been blasted along the southern slope of the ridge looked to provide some cover. He decided to use it to bypass the Italians on Mount Kuk and led his men in a dash along it. The Rommel Detachment had now got itself behind the Italian defensive line on the ridge and soon encountered groups of enemy totally surprised by its appearance. He came upon a road running up a valley that was clearly being used for resupply. He set up a position astride it. Trucks began to fall into his hands, including some with very welcome food for his men. A large column of men then approached. Rommel had only 150 men with him and tried to persuade the Italians to surrender by waving a white handkerchief and sending an officer wearing a white armband to parley with them. He was immediately seized, and the Italians opened fire. After some ten minutes, however, they laid down their arms and a *bersaglieri* (light infantry) brigade, 2,000 men strong, fell into Rommel's hands. The day was now far advanced, so the detachment moved down into a village and there met up with the remainder of the battalion.

Two mountains—Mounts Cragonza and Mrzli—still barred the way to Mount Matajur and needed to be taken to reach the final objective. Rommel was not prepared to delay. Having been reinforced by additional companies, he set off for Mount Cragonza once darkness had fallen. En route lay the village of Jevszek, which he knew to be occupied by Italian troops. He therefore skirted round it and then paused. Just before dawn he set out toward the summit of Mount Cragonza, leaving one company to take care of the village, which it did, netting another thousand prisoners. Rommel and the rest of his detachment quickly found themselves under fire from

Cragonza once daylight came. He saw no alternative but to make a frontal attack even though there was no cover. Drive and determination spurred them on, and by 7:15 A.M. the mountain was in their hands. With little pause Rommel now arranged for the supporting artillery to fire on Mount Mrzli. This time he decided to use his white handkerchief ruse again, and it worked. Another 1,500 prisoners were added to his haul.

Now Mount Matajur lay in Rommel's sights, but as he prepared to attack it, he received orders from his battalion commander to withdraw. Major Theodor Sprösser assumed from the number of prisoners Rommel had captured that the peak had been secured and the battle was over. Some of Rommel's companies had already begun to pull back on Sprösser's orders, but Rommel was not to be denied the final prize. Even though he now had only a hundred men and six machine guns still immediately available, he chose to ignore Sprösser's order. His machine guns laid down a barrage, and he began to advance. There was, however, no return fire, and soon the Italians began to lay down their arms. Continuing to press on upward, Rommel's men reached the summit of Mount Matajur at 11:40 A.M. on October 26, 1917, and he fired flares to signal his success. The Rommel detachment had been in continuous action for over fifty hours. It had taken some 9,000 prisoners while its own casualties had been a mere 36 killed and wounded. Rommel's men were singled out for mention in an Alpine Corps order of the day, but Rommel himself received no individual award for his remarkable exploits.

By now the Italian defenses had been broken and soldiers were streaming to the rear. Rommel's battalion followed them up, crossing the River Tagliamento and heading for the Piave. At one point Rommel was ordered to force a pass. It was after nightfall before his troops were in position after an exhausting climb. Success depended on the synchronization of the supporting machine-gun fire with the movement of the assault troops, but the latter failed to attack at the right moment because they expected Rommel to be with them at H-hour, while he admitted to have lingered too long with his machine guns. The result was that the attack was repulsed. Rommel felt his first failure very deeply, but daylight revealed that the Italians had withdrawn from the pass. The advance could continue. Eventually, on November 9, they reached the Piave opposite Longarone. Rommel was leading the advance guard but had with him just ten men on captured bicycles. He could see Italian troops withdrawing on the road running south of Longarone and parallel with the river. He engaged them with long-range rifle fire. He and his small group then managed to get across the river south of Longerone and establish a blocking position, and soon he was taking prisoners. The rest of his command, two rifle companies and one machine company, joined him.

Rommel knew that Longarone was full of Italian troops and was determined to capture it. Since the light was now fast fading, it would have to be another night attack, with support being provided by machine guns from across the river. Just as he reached the outskirts of the town, the Italians opened fire. At the same time the German machine guns opened up from his right flank, but the fire was falling behind his men—another failure in coordination. As he tried to extricate his troops, a mass of Italians rushed southward down the road, knocking the Germans aside and almost capturing Rommel. He set off cross-country at a run and managed to reach a small detachment that he had positioned on the road to prevent any northward movement by Italian reinforcements. He quickly got them to face about, just in time to meet the Italian onrush. German reinforcements now arrived, and the Italians withdrew into the town. With the arrival of daylight Rommel advanced once more on Longarone and was greeted by a German officer who had recently fallen into Italian hands. He was accompanied by a crowd of handkerchief-waving Italians and bore a letter of surrender from the commandant of Longarone. Rommel and his men then entered the town to a warm welcome from the local inhabitants.

The Württembergers continued to advance southward along the line of the Upper Piave, but the offensive was beginning to run out of momentum and was held on the lower Piave. British and French troops also began to arrive to help shore up the Italian defenses. Rommel's battalion spent Christmas near Feltre, and a welcome present was the award of Prussia's highest decoration, the Pour le Mérite, to Major Sprösser and himself. Then it was back to the front line. As a result of a successful attack by French mountain troops, the line in the Württembergers' sector was withdrawn northward one and a half miles. They were the rearguard and had to cope with a spirited attack before pulling back on the night of January 1, 1918. A week later Rommel and Sprösser left their battalion to go on leave.

Rommel was fated not to return to the Württemberg Mountain Battalion. Instead he was appointed to the staff of LXIV Corps on the Western Front. He remained a staff officer throughout the remainder of the war, but, for a man of action, as he now demonstrably was, it was not a post that he enjoyed. Indeed, he yearned to be with his old battalion, also deployed to the Western Front, and constantly followed its fortunes, but with a "heavy heart" as its casualties mounted during the grim battles of the summer and autumn 1918.[4]

The November 1918 armistice and its aftermath was a depressing time for the German officer corps. It saw the kaiser forced into exile in Holland and some units taken over by soldiers' councils, echoing what had happened to the Russian army the previous year during Bolshevik Revolution. Germany itself appeared in imminent danger of being taken over by the Communists, and the new republican government appeared unable to cope with the growing unrest. Meanwhile, under the terms of the armistice, the German armies in France withdrew in good order back over the Rhine. The Allied armies followed up and established bridgeheads over the river.

Matters went from bad to worse. By the beginning of 1919 civil war had erupted in Berlin and other parts of the country as the Communists and their allies tussled with government troops and the Freikorps, groups of recently discharged soldiers who had banded together to fight the Communists. Captain Rommel himself was soon removed from his staff post, probably to his relief, and returned to his parent regiment, the 124th Infantry Regiment, at the end of 1918. March 1919 found him commanding an internal security company at Friedrichshafen. His men were sailors toying, like many in the armed forces, with the idea of revolution, but Rommel appears to have asserted his personality and instilled some discipline. The local area remained quiet, but in March 1920 Rommel and his command did become involved with unrest.

The Treaty of Versailles, which formally brought Germany's war to an end, was very severe in its terms. The financial compensation that the country was forced to pay for the material damage that it had caused would soon bring an economic crisis. The loss of its overseas possessions also rankled, but even more so did the physical severing of East Prussia from the remainder of the country in order to create access to the sea for the newly independent state of Poland. There were also the severe restrictions on the armed forces, and the army was reduced to a mere 100,000 men, insufficient to defend Germany's borders. Right-wing elements in the country were furious and blamed the government. A group of officers and Freikorps men resolved to overthrow it and hold fresh elections. They were led by Wolfgang Kapp, a right-wing politician, and the commander of the Berlin garrison. Matters came to a head when the Inter-Allied Military Control Commission, responsible for seeing that the German armed forces honored the Versailles terms, ordered the disbandment of two Freikorps. General Walther von Luttwitz, the Berlin garrison commander, refused and, in spite of the government ordering his arrest, led his men into Berlin on March 13, 1920. They were greeted by a crowd of supporters. The head of the armed forces, General Hans von Seekt, had no wish to see German soldier firing on German solider and ordered the army not to intervene. The government retired to Dresden, and Kapp tried to grab the reins of power. The trade unions called a general strike in protest, and Kapp and Luttwitz were forced to flee Berlin. Taking advantage of the apparent political vacuum, the Communists staged uprisings in the Ruhr, Germany's western industrial region, and other areas. These were speedily put down by the army, including Rommel's company, which was sent to Westphalia. There is no record of what Rommel thought of it all, but certainly at that time he would have believed that a soldier is a servant of the state and should not become involved in politics.

The severe reduction in the size of the German army meant that only the cream of the officer corps was retained. Not surprisingly, in view of his outstanding combat record, Rommel was one of the lucky ones. On October 1, 1920, he was posted to Stuttgart to command a rifle company in the 13th Infantry Regiment. This was to be his home for the next nine years. For him it was a period of introspection during which Germany went through a severe economic crisis. Rommel concentrated on training his men. Physical fitness was particularly high in his priorities. He qualified as a ski instructor, teaching not only the men of his regiment, but those of other units as well. He also took his wife on skiing, cycling, and hiking trips, on one occasion to Italy to visit the scenes of his exploits in 1917. He was highly regarded by all ranks. Reporting on him in 1929, his battalion commander described Rommel as "a quiet, sterling character, always tactful in his manner," but with "great military gifts," especially in his eye for terrain. The report also recommended Rommel for instructional duties, and this was to be his next posting.[5]

In September 1929 Rommel became an instructor at the Infantry School at Dresden. His main task was training officer candidates, and he soon became their hero. His lectures often included descriptions of his own battles as a way of drawing out tactical lessons. In particular he drummed home the importance of avoiding unnecessary casualties, emphasizing the need to dig in as soon as the unit halted. He became, in the words of the senior instructor at the school, "a towering personality."[6] Promoted to major in 1932, Rommel's efforts were rewarded the following year when he was given command of a battalion. By that time Germany had undergone a dramatic transformation.

Economic recovery during the second half of the 1920s had reduced political tensions, but Germany, like many other countries, was badly hit by the 1929 Wall Street crash. There was an upsurge of political unrest as Adolf Hitler's National Socialists clashed with the Communists. Hitler, however, was determined to gain power through the ballot box, and was steadily gaining votes. In the March 1932 presidential elections he came in second, behind the venerable Field Marshal Paul von Hindenburg, gaining 30 percent of the votes cast.

Because Hindenburg failed narrowly to secure 50 percent of the vote, there was a run off the following month, with Hitler increasing his share to 37 percent of the vote after one of the other candidates dropped out. The general election held later that summer saw the Nazis gain the largest number of seats in the Reichstag, but not enough to form a government on their own. Hitler would not share power with others, and so another election had to be held that November. The Nazi share of seats fell slightly, mainly because of improvements in the economic situation. Even so, they still had the largest number, and after a considerable amount of political jockeying, Hindenburg appointed Hitler chancellor in January 1933. In his original cabinet there were only two other National Socialists, and the moderates within in it hoped that they could isolate him. Hitler, however, summoned fresh elections for early March. On the eve of the ballot there was a fire at the Reichstag. Hitler blamed the Communists, claiming that they were preparing an uprising. He persuaded Hindenburg to issue a decree restricting civil and political liberties. The elections that followed still did not give the Nazis a majority, but Hitler then steered through legislation that enabled him to do what he liked to consolidate his power. Within a few months political opposition to the Nazis became illegal, and Germany was a dictatorship.

The political turmoil that Germany had suffered largely passed the apolitical Rommel by. Like most of those in the armed forces, he certainly welcomed Hitler's plans to expand them, but his attention was now concentrated on his new command. The 3rd (Jäger) Battalion of the 17th Infantry Regiment was a light infantry battalion based at Goslar in the Harz Mountains. With his love of outdoor pursuits, the location suited Rommel perfectly. As was in his nature, he led from the front and established himself from his very first day in command. To test Rommel's mettle his officers invited him to climb a local mountain and then ski down it. They all did this three times, and when Rommel suggested that they accompany him on a fourth ascent, they realized they had met their match.

It was at Goslar that Rommel met Hitler for the first time. The German leader visited the town in September 1934, and Rommel's battalion supplied an honor guard. By this time the army had to be grateful to Hitler. His political shock troops, the *Sturmabteilung* (SA) in their brown uniforms, had become so much a part of the scenery that Ernst Röhm, their leader, believed that they, and not the army, should have responsibility for the defense of Germany. General Werner von Blomberg, the defense minister, drew Hitler's attention to this challenge. At the same time, and to demonstrate the army's loyalty, he ordered all ranks to wear the *Hoheitsabzeichen*, the new national emblem of eagle and swastika, above the right breast pocket of their uniforms. He also began to implement Hitler's anti-Jewish measures, weeding out officers of non-Aryan descent, although war veterans were at this stage exempt. Impressed by this action, Hitler called a meeting of SA leaders and army commanders at the end of February 1934. He confirmed the primacy of the army, although the SA would be allowed to carry out some military training and would help defend Germany's eastern frontier, and he made Blomberg and Röhm sign an agreement to this effect. But it soon leaked out that Röhm had no intention of honoring this agreement. Hitler realized then that the SA leader was getting above himself. The result was that on the night of June 30, 1934, Hitler sent out his henchmen to murder Röhm and other senior SA men. What became known as the Night of the Long Knives was also used by Hitler's subordinates to settle old scores. The deaths of two generals, both of whom, it is true, had been involved in politics, did cause some unease in the army. Blomberg, however, was grateful to Hitler for having removed the SA threat without the army having to dirty its hands. There was, though, a price to pay. Hindenburg died at the beginning of August 1934, and Hitler now insisted that every member of the armed forces take an oath of loyalty to him personally rather than to the state, as had been the case.

All this would have been in Rommel's mind when he met Hitler at Goslar, but like his brother officers he accepted the new oath. His time with his unit was, however, limited to just two years. In September 1935 he was posted as an instructor to the War Academy at Potsdam. Once again he excelled, and he now came into close contact with Hitler. In September 1936 he was attached to Hitler's escort for the annual Nuremberg rally and received the Führer's personal thanks. While at Potsdam he also worked his lectures on his World War I combat experiences into a book. *Infantry Attacks* was published in 1937 and, to Rommel's surprise, became a bestseller. Hitler certainly read it. Its author was canny when it came to royalties, however. He instructed his publisher to pay him just a fixed sum from his royalties each year so as to avoid paying a heavy tax on his earnings.

Rommel was also making his mark on German youth, and in February 1937 was appointed the army's liaison officer to Baldur von Shirach, leader of the Hitler Youth. At the time, the organization concentrated upon sport, culture, and National Socialist indoctrination, but the War Ministry wanted to introduce paramilitary training as well to prepare the boys for military service. It is clear that Rommel and Shirach had very different views and did not get along personally. The latter had not received any military training and was eleven years younger than Rommel. Shirach found Rommel's stories of his exploits tedious and resented that he used them to create hero worship of himself among the Hitler Youth. At the same time Shirach accused Rommel of wanting to give military training priority over the boys' education. Yet Rommel's supporters asserted that he thought quite the opposite and believed that Shirach placed too much emphasis on paramilitary activities and sport at the expense of his charges' schooling. Whatever the truth, Rommel's part-time attachment to the Hitler Youth was terminated, leaving him to concentrate wholly on his teaching at the War Academy. But even though he had fallen foul of one of Hitler's favorites, the Führer still needed his services.

Apart from the rapid expansion of the German armed forces, the years 1936–1938 saw the country increasingly flexing its muscles. This began in March 1936 when Hitler broke the last shackle of Versailles by marching his troops into the demilitarized Rhineland. This was a gamble. The army was still undergoing a rapid expansion, and little of it was operationally prepared should the French and British choose to oppose the move, which they did not. Hitler's next target was Austria. He struck in March 1938 and again achieved a bloodless coup and incorporated that country into the Third Reich. There is no doubt that Rommel, like many others of his countrymen, was impressed by Hitler's boldness. While he was not a Nazi per se, Rommel did attend indoctrination courses and clearly supported many of the National Socialist objectives. As a patriot he was fully behind Hitler's aim to make Germany great again, especially by restoring its pre-1914 borders. The social reforms designed to restore full employment also met with his approval. All this outweighed the often thuggish behavior of the SS and SA. As for the Jews, Rommel had no personal enmity toward them, but he did understand that there was a question over their divided loyalties. He also supported Hitler's demand that his soldiers should be political and be prepared to fight for National Socialist policies. Yet Rommel saw this in the context of motivating his soldiers rather than making them into Nazis. Like his peers, he had sworn an oath of personal loyalty to Hitler, and in the German military code such an oath could not be broken. It was very much "My country, right or wrong," and raises a question about the degree to which soldiers of any country, as servants of the state, should support a regime that clearly has an evil streak in it.

Now Hitler turned his eyes on Czechoslovakia, his southeastern neighbor and a Versailles creation that he regarded as an aberration. His initial target was the westernmost province of the Sudetenland, which contained a sizable German minority. The high command of the German army was generally aghast, since the Czechs had strong defenses and any military move against them might well bring in France and Britain. Besides which, they did not consider that the Wehrmacht was yet ready for war. While Hitler held off during the summer of 1938, he declared that the Czechs must hand the Sudetenland over by October 1 or he would use force. The Western democracies still hoped that the appeasement of Hitler would avoid another major conflict in Europe, and when Hitler declared in September that, once he had secured the Sudetenland, Germany's territorial expansion was at an end, they believed him. The Czechs, realizing that they could now expect no military support, caved in, and on October 1 German troops entered the province. Rommel's part in this coup was to command Hitler's escort battalion, once more bringing him to the notice of the Führer.

In November 1938 Rommel left Potsdam for a new posting. He had been appointed to command the War Academy at Wiener Neustadt, south of Vienna. This assignment signified that the Austrian army existed no more and was now part of the German army. Hitler, however, was not yet finished with his territorial expansion or with Rommel. March 1939 witnessed the dismemberment of the rump of Czechoslovakia. Hitler summoned Rommel once more to command his escort. The two met at the Czech border in a blizzard. The SS escort had not arrived, and Hitler wondered what to do. Rommel urged him to drive straight to Prague and said that he would personally protect him. Hitler agreed, and they made their way to Hradcany Castle, the seat of the president of the country. This action reflected in both Hitler and Rommel the same quality of boldness. Later that month the two also entered the port of Memel (now Klaipeda), which had been taken away from Germany under the Versailles Treaty and annexed by Lithuania in 1923. Thereafter Rommel returned to Wiener Neustadt to continue training his officer cadets.

Hitler, however, still had one further item on his expansionist agenda: the hated Polish Corridor, a strip of territory given to Poland under the Versailles Treaty to provide the new state access to the Baltic Sea through the port of Danzig (Gdansk). The Corridor physically severed East Prussia from the remainder of Germany. In 1934 Hitler had signed a ten-year nonaggression pact with the Poles, both to disguise his intentions over the Corridor and to draw Poland away from its alliance with France. In October 1938 he demanded that the Poles restore Danzig to Germany and allow the construction of road and rail links to East Prussia across the Corridor. The Poles refused and did so again in March 1939. Then, at the end of April, Hitler reiterated his demands and stated that the nonaggression pact was at an end. It was at this point that Britain and France finally realized that war was inevitable. Rommel, too, recognized that Polish intransigence meant that Hitler would have to invade. Both he and Lucie had fond memories of Danzig and wanted to see it back in the German fold. The question in Rommel's mind, though, was whether there would be a role for him.

He had his suspicions that he would once more be close to Hitler, and he was right. On August 22 he was ordered to Berlin and told that he would command Hitler's field headquarters. The headquarters was a train called *Amerika,* protected by four antitank guns and twelve 20mm Flak guns, with a unit of some 380 men. Rommel was also delighted that Hitler had him promoted to major general, backdated to June 1, 1939. The invasion itself was scheduled to take place at dawn on August 26, and Rommel believed that Poland would be defeated within two weeks, especially since a great diplomatic coup had been achieved in the signing of a nonaggression pact with the Soviet Union on the twenty-third. He also thought that Britain and France were unlikely to come to Poland's aid.

He was wrong. The Western democracies made it plain that they would help the Poles if they were attacked. Furthermore, it was expected that Italy would join Germany in the war under the Pact of Steel that the two countries had signed in May 1939. Benito Mussolini, the Italian dictator, stated, however, that his country was not ready for war. This announcement threw Hitler into a state of turmoil. The invasion was postponed literally hours before it was due to begin, and to compensate for the lack of Italian support some frantic diplomacy took place to try to persuade Britain to break its tie with Poland. For Rommel, as with the troops positioned close to the Polish border, it was a time of frustration, although he did his best to curb his impatience. "Waiting is a bore," he wrote to Lucie, "but it can't be helped."[7]

The diplomatic efforts proved fruitless, and on August 31 Rommel was informed that the invasion would now take place at 4:50 A.M. the next day. And so it happened, with a faked border incident to justify to the outside world that Poland was the aggressor. In the south, Gerd von Rundstedt's Army Group South attacked from north of the Carpathian Mountains, while Fedor von Bock's Army Group North overran the Corridor. Then both army groups would converge on Warsaw. Not, however, until the evening of September 3 did Hitler board his train. By then Britain and France had issued ultimatums demanding that Hitler withdraw his forces from Poland. He refused, and the two countries declared war on Germany. Fears that they might launch an immediate offensive were soon dispelled, however. True, the French did begin a cautious advance into the Saarland on September 7, but they were not prepared to move beyond the guns of the Maginot Line on which the defense of the country was based. It was the beginning of what became known as the Phony War in the West.

Rommel was a mere bystander, but a very privileged one. Hitler was keen to see everything going on and toured every part of the front as the cream of the new German Army, its panzer or armored formations plunged ever deeper into Poland, creating large pockets of still-resisting Polish troops, which were reduced by the follow-up infantry. It was the conduct of this new form of high-speed warfare, which the Germans termed "*Blitzkrieg*," or lightning war, that impressed Rommel. The concentration of force, shock, and surprise, combined with flanking moves so as to strike the enemy from an unexpected direction, reflected exactly the type of tactics that he had employed with his mountain troops nearly twenty-five years earlier. The fact that the tanks had armored protection for their crews was a bonus that his Württembergers had not enjoyed.

The Polish campaign drew Rommel even closer to Hitler. Spending so many hours in his company was exhilarating. There was already a bond between them: Hitler, too, had been a decorated *Frontsoldat* during World War I. Rommel was also present at Hitler's daily conferences, and they gave him an insight into the higher direction of the war.

On September 17 any remaining hopes that the Poles had of holding out were dashed when the Russians, under a pre-agreed arrangement, attacked from the east. Two days later Rommel accompanied Hitler to Danzig to celebrate its liberation. By now Warsaw, under siege, was being pounded from the air and the ground. The end of the war was in sight. Hitler returned to Berlin, and Rommel was allowed a few days' leave in Wiener Neustadt. Then he flew to Warsaw, which had fallen on September 27, to arrange for the German victory parade. He was horrified by the destruction caused by the German siege, but his view was that the damage would have been even more severe if it had continued longer and that Warsaw's inhabitants were probably relieved that the city had surrendered relatively quickly. The parade itself took place on October 5, after Rommel had paid a brief visit to Berlin.

Hitler had expressed his intention to his generals to turn immediately on France, but first he made peace overtures, offering terms to both France and Britain if they would respect the new state of affairs in Eastern Europe. The olive branch was dismissed out of hand, and so on October 9 Hitler issued a directive for an attack in the West. Belgian neutrality was to be ignored, as it had been in 1914, but this time the Netherlands was also to be invaded. He wanted the attack to be launched in November, before the Western allies grew too strong, but his generals were not so keen. They wanted more time to assimilate the lessons of the Polish campaign and to prepare for an assault against an enemy significantly more formidable than the Poles had been. On November 23 an exasperated Hitler summoned them to the Chancellery and told them what he thought of them. Rommel was present. He wrote to Lucie: "The Führer didn't mince his language. But it seemed to me to have been highly necessary, because when I speak with my fellow generals I rarely find one who supports him body and soul."[8] Winter now took hold, and it was a severe one in Western Europe, so the Phony War continued.

Rommel himself was understandably frustrated, as his letters to Lucie imply. Apart from attending Hitler's daily conferences on the war, there was little for him to do. He wanted to take a more active part and was conscious that it had now been a few years since he had held a field command. He began to drop hints to Hitler, and the latter agreed that he could have a division. In view of his past experience the powers that be thought that a mountain division would be the most suitable. Rommel was not satisfied; it was a panzer division he wanted, and he told Hitler so. The authorities would not back down, pointing out that Rommel had no experience other than the infantry. Hitler insisted, and eventually, on February 6, 1940, Rommel was informed by telegram that he was to take command of the 7th Panzer Division. Now he could once more put into practice his unique style of command.

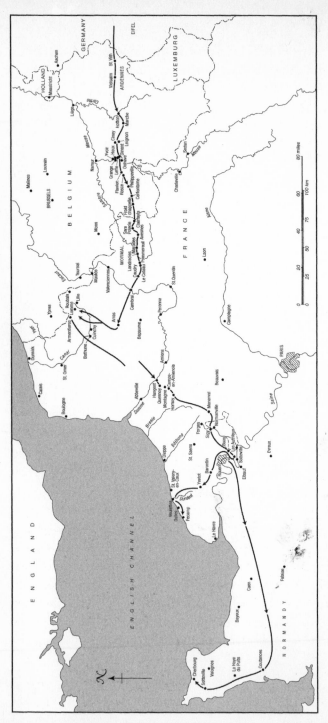

The Path of 7th Panzer Division May–June 1940. Map by David Hoxley.

CHAPTER 2

France 1940

ON FEBRUARY 10, 1940, ROMMEL ARRIVED AT BAD
Godesberg on the River Rhine to take command of the 7th
Panzer Division. His predecessor with the 7th, Georg
Stumme, had been promoted to command of a corps. (Their
paths would briefly cross again.) The 7th had been formed in
1938 as the 2nd Light Division, whose purpose was medium-
range reconnaissance. The Polish campaign had demonstrated
that such light divisions were too cumbersome to carry out
their role and lacked the punch to be capable of much else.
They were therefore converted to panzer divisions. A light division had comprised one tank battalion, two mechanized cavalry regiments, and a reconnaissance battalion; the new panzer
division had fewer tanks than the original panzer divisions and

possessed one three-battalion regiment (as opposed to two two-battalion regiments).

A week later Rommel returned to Berlin to have a farewell lunch with Hitler, who presented him with a copy of *Mein Kampf*, inscribed "To General Rommel with pleasant memories." He visited his publisher in Potsdam to pick up copies of his own book for his subordinates to read and then returned to Bad Godesberg to lick his division into shape. He was not initially impressed with what he saw. Half of his 218 tanks were Czech 38t models. While these had a useful 37mm gun and good mobility, their armored protection was not up to that of the Pzkw III and IV, of which his panzer regiment had a number. The 7th Panzer Division also had two motorized rifle battalions of three battalions each, a reconnaissance battalion with armored cars, a motorcycle battalion, an engineer battalion, 75 artillery pieces organized in nine batteries, and an antitank battalion.

While he got on well with Colonel Karl Rothenburg, a tough ex-policeman who commanded the panzer regiment and had also won the Pour le Mérite as an infantryman during World War I, he was not impressed with some of his other officers. He felt that they had become soft with comfortable living, and so he personally set an example by going for a run at 6:00 A.M. each morning. Rommel was using the technique he had employed at Goslar. Leadership by example and never expecting his men to do anything that he was not capable of doing himself were characteristics of his style. Leading from the front was and is a very good quality in a junior officer, but at higher levels of command it can degrade an officer's effectiveness. It can lead to over-supervision, as often happened in Vietnam when senior commanders tried to directly control operations at the lowest level through the use of command helicopters. Rommel always wanted to be at the critical point of the battlefield, and he usually got away with it through sheer personality and charisma. His style did, however, create difficulties for his staff, who sometimes were unable to contact him. He also quickly sacked one battalion commander who did not meet his standards. "Word of this rapid firing will soon get around and some of the others will pull their socks up," he commented.[1] He also thought that most of his officers were generally politically ambivalent and in some cases openly critical of the Nazi regime. The posting to the division of a few high-ranking Nazis, including a senior aide to propaganda minister Joseph Goebbels and the chief editor of the virulent anti-Jewish newspaper *Der Stürmer,* quickly caused them to be more circumspect.

Rommel clearly needed to get to grips with armored warfare. He did this by sending his regimental commanders on leave and spending his days with the troops. Soon he was taking elements of the division on cross-country marches and experimenting with ways in which shock and surprise could be created. He also firmly believed that junior officers must be allowed to use their initiative. He gave them numerous lectures on tactics and how he wanted the division to operate so that they could get inside his mind-set. It was the same with the divisional staff. Rommel's instinct, as it had always been, was to spend as much time as possible with his forward troops so that he could get a sense of the battle. He decided to travel in a converted tank or armored car with, when possible, a signals vehicle to ensure communications with his headquarters. He accepted, though, that there was always a danger that he might not be able to appreciate the bigger picture, and so his staff needed to have a full understanding of the situation at all times and to be prepared to countermand his orders if they felt that there were important factors of which he was unaware.

While Rommel was immersing himself in learning how to handle a panzer division, the German plan for the invasion of the West had undergone radical changes. The original *Fall Gelb* (Case Yellow) envisaged a Schlieffen-like wheel, as used by the Germans in 1914, to bring the British and French armies to battle and defeat them. Fedor von Bock's Army Group B would be in the north and Gerd von Rundstedt's Army Group A to its south. Army Group C under Ritter von Leeb would be responsible for masking the Maginot Line, the defensive fortifications the French had built to protect its eastern borders. A revised plan was issued at the end of October 1939 that called for an advance on a broader front with Army Group B still taking the principal role and Army Group A expected to protect its right flank. The overall aim, namely, to occupy much of the Low Countries and northern France as quickly as possible so that a successful sea and air campaign could be waged against Britain, remained in place. Rundstedt and, more notably, his astute chief of staff, Erich von Manstein, were not happy with the plan. They considered the overall aim to be far too limited; the total defeat of France was essential. Furthermore, the fortifications and waterways that Bock faced in Belgium favored the defense, which, in any event he would be meeting head on. Rather, Rundstedt and Manstein argued, it was Army Group A that should have the decisive role; it should advance through the wooded Ardennes and then cut off the Allied armies in the north before the German armies turned on the rest of France.

The alternative proposal initially fell on deaf ears. Indeed, in early January, and encouraged by favorable long-range weather forecasts, Hitler decreed that the attack would be launched on the seventeenth of the month using the existing plan. No sooner had he done so than a German light aircraft carrying a Luftwaffe staff officer made a forced landing in Belgium. He was carrying some details of the plan, which he tried to burn, but the Belgian authorities were able to seize the charred remnants. Not knowing how much the Belgians had learned, Hitler put the operation on hold. This gave Rundstedt and Manstein more time to advance their plan, although the latter was soon posted to command an infantry corps, probably because he had become too much of a thorn in the flesh of the high command. By strange coincidence, together with three other newly appointed corps commanders, Manstein was present at Hitler's farewell lunch for Rommel on February 17. After lunch, he presented his plan to Hitler, though Rommel had departed by then. Hitler accepted the plan, and within a week it had been disseminated down to army commander level.

Under the new plan Rundstedt's army group was considerably reinforced. In particular, it now had the bulk of the armor—seven panzer and three motorized divisions—compared with Bock's three panzer and one motorized divisions. The bulk was organized as a panzer group under Ewald von Kleist, a bold cavalryman, and consisted of two panzer corps (XIX and XLI), and a motorized corps. Rommel's 7th Panzer Division was to be under Hermann Hoth's XV Panzer Corps, together with the 5th Panzer Division. Hoth's corps was under the command of the German Fourth Army and would cover the northern flank of Panzer Group Kleist. Hoth was specifically tasked with crossing the Meuse north of Dinant as his first objective. To his south Georg-Hans Reinhardt's XLI Panzer Corps would cross at Monthermé, and XIX Panzer Corps, under Heinz Guderian, the driving force behind the German style of armored warfare, would cross at Sedan. It meant that all the panzer divisions needed to be thoroughly rehearsed in river crossings, so they carried out training on the River Mosel.

Both German and Allied attention was diverted in early April 1940 by the German invasion of Denmark and Norway, and it was not until April 30 that Hitler ordered that his forces be ready to strike any time after May 5. Uncertain weather caused further slight postponement, but finally, on the evening of May 9, the code word "Danzig" was issued. The invasion of the West would take place at dawn next day. Rommel scribbled a quick line to Lucie: "We're packing up at last. You'll get all the news for the next few days from the papers. Don't worry yourself. Everything will go alright."[2]

The XV Panzer Corps advanced into Belgium with the 5th Panzer Division to the north and Rommel's division on its left. Where opposition was met, Rommel quickly learned that firing his guns soon suppressed it. Indeed, his troops made much use of preventative fire, spraying woods and other possible enemy positions as they passed. Even so, Rommel was concerned that they were behind schedule. They passed through St. Vith and Vielsalm, the names that would become well known to the U.S. troops fighting in this area four and a half years later, and reached the River Ourthe at Hotton by midday on May 11, by which time the division had advanced forty miles. Pushing his men on for all he was worth, Rommel was soon getting well ahead of his sister panzer division. Recognizing this fact and with the need to establish crossings over the Meuse as soon as possible, Hoth gave Rommel the 31st Panzer Regiment from the 5th Panzer Division. This added unit increased his frontage but gave him more scope for maneuver. He was clearly elated by the confidence Hoth had in him and wrote another quick note to Lucie: "Everything wonderful so far. Am way ahead of my neighbors. I'm completely hoarse from orders and shouting. Had a bare three hours' sleep and an occasional meal. Otherwise I'm absolutely fine."[3]

The 7th Panzer Division reached Dinant on the afternoon of May 12, having traveled sixty-five miles from their starting point. The bridges over the Meuse had been blown, but by last light Rommel had the east bank secured. His motorcycle battalion now showed initiative. Scouting northward they came to the village of Houx, where they noted a small island in the middle of the river connected to the home bank by a stone weir. Dismounting, a group scrambled across the weir, got onto the island, which was undefended, and reached the west bank of the river by means of a lock gate. Soon they were reinforced by elements of the 7th Rifle Regiment. The French, who were positioned on high ground back from the river, woke up to what was happening and subjected the small bridgehead to heavy fire. Casualties mounted, and attempts to cross by rubber boat by Dinant itself were also thwarted. By now it was the early hours of the thirteenth. Rommel came to see for himself and recognized that the river was too much in view of the French. His guns did not have smoke shells, so he ordered a number of houses to be set on fire to provide some cover from view. He drove back to his headquarters to meet Hoth and the army commander, Hans Günther von Kluge, and explained the situation to them. He then returned to the river north of Dinant. Dismounting from his vehicle, he and his adjutant, Major Schraepler, dashed to another weir that had been identified at Leffe, having ordered some tanks and two field guns to meet him there. Rommel and Schraepler climbed on board one of the tanks and moved back to Dinant. The French fire was heavy, and Schraepler was wounded in the arm. Rommel ordered other tanks to drive northward along the road bordering the river and to fire at the French as they did so. He led them up to Houx and organized another battalion of the 7th Rifle Regiment to cross in rubber boats. Typically, he jumped into one of the lead boats. Once across he organized the defense of the bridgehead, steadying the men when the French put in a halfhearted counterattack with tanks. Then he was supervising the construction of bridges so that his tanks could get across. He seemed to be everywhere with his own sense of urgency, inspiring everyone to greater effort. There is no doubt that his leadership had a significant effect on the crossing of the Meuse and, as we shall see, he continued to command in this way. Nowadays, with greatly improved radio communications, as well as computer technology, the need for a higher commander to lead from the front is less necessary at the height of a battle. He is better employed at his headquarters, where he can see the big picture to a much greater extent than Rommel could in 1940. It does not absolve him, however, from getting out among his troops when there is a lull.

By 9:00 A.M. on May 14 Rommel had some thirty tanks of the 25th Panzer Regiment across the river. He was with them in his own tank and wanted to concentrate them in a wood to prepare for the next phase. In carrying out this maneuver his tank was hit, slid down a slope, and ended up at the bottom with its turret jammed. Bleeding from a splinter wound, Rommel and the crew clambered out and made for his signals vehicle, but it had also been hit and immobilized. Eventually they were rescued by Rothenburg in his command tank. Even so, by the end of the day the bridgeheads were secure, as were those of the other panzer corps. The next step was to advance out of the bridgehead and break through the Maginot Line extension, which, in fact, was little more than a thin line of pillboxes and antitank obstacles and nothing like the formidable fortifications of the main Maginot Line.

Rommel's orders for May 15 were simple. The 25th Panzer Regiment was to lead the division westward through Philippeville to the village of Cerfontaine, twenty-five miles from the Meuse. He emphasized that the momentum of the advance had to be maintained and there could not be any halts. Preventative fire was again to be used, both by the artillery engaging potential targets on the flanks off the map and by the tanks themselves firing on the move. He would also have the support of Ju87 Stuka dive-bombers. Rommel himself accompanied the tanks with his small tactical command group. They had a brush with French tanks and then moved in column through the wood toward Philippeville. Abandoned French vehicles, weapons, and equipment littered the route. The French troops themselves fled when they heard the noise of the tanks or were attacked by the Stukas. There was a brief fight with troops holding high ground to the northwest of Philippeville, but otherwise the opposition was sparse, and Cerfontaine was soon reached. One factor behind the division's success was that Rommel ordered situation reports to be sent by radio in clear, which saved time and kept both the divisional staff and the artillery fully abreast of what was going on. Rommel himself returned to bring up his infantry, since it had been slow to get moving and had allowed enemy troops to infiltrate the resultant gap between it and the tanks. Rommel was not best pleased by this, commenting that "the officers of a Panzer division must learn to think and act independently within the framework of the general plan and not wait until they receive orders."[4]

The next day would see the 7th Panzer Division pass into France and deal with the Maginot Line extension. Rommel's plan was much more carefully thought out this time. His tanks would advance in extended order and halt when they came up against the fortifications. His two infantry regiments, controlled by a brigade headquarters especially established for the purpose, would then break through, supported by all his artillery and the tank guns, after which the tanks would resume the lead. He himself would travel in Rothenburg's tank, but was ordered by Hoth to remain at his divisional headquarters for the time being. The reason was a visit by Kluge, who expressed surprise that the advance had not begun but appeared satisfied once Rommel explained his plan. Crossing the frontier, Rommel used his engineers to deal with the first vestiges of the Maginot Line extension, a pillbox and an anti-tank hedgehog (a collection of obstacles made from angled iron). Although there was now some French fire, Rommel began to sense that the defenses were not as extensive as he had feared. He therefore ordered his tanks to advance at full speed, spraying fire as they went. It worked, and in no time at all they were through. Once again Rommel had demonstrated the value of a commander being well forward, but there was a penalty to be paid. As the tanks pressed onward toward the day's ultimate objective, Avesnes, Rommel's radio communications with his rear began to fade with increasing distance from division. A crisis arose when a French tank battalion was reported in Avesnes, which the leading panzer battalion, Rommel still with it, had bypassed. He could not contact his headquarters, and so had to send back some of his lead tanks to deal with it. Yet Rommel was still keen to keeping pressing forward, as aware as he was of the growing French confusion.

Indeed, by this stage the Allied plans were already in disarray. Their northern armies, including the British Expeditionary Force (BEF), had advanced into Belgium and taken up position on the River Dyle, since it offered a better scope for defense than the terrain along the north part of the Franco-Belgian border. By May 16, with the panzer thrust through the defenses on the Meuse and the French Ninth Army, which had tried to oppose it, in a state of disintegration, the Allied high command began to realize the danger of its northern armies being cut off. They were therefore ordered to withdraw from Belgium in the face of Army Group B.

It was against this backdrop that Rommel, with little pause, fixed his eyes on what he saw as his next objective, to achieve crossings over the River Sambre. Lack of radio communication meant that he could not get this plan cleared by Hoth, and his tanks, which were especially short of ammunition, had not been resupplied. Nevertheless, Rommel resumed his advance at 4:00 A.M. on May 17 with little besides his tanks. They passed through Landrecies, which was packed with bewildered French troops as well as refugees. Rommel had to detach elements to disarm them and send them eastward, and after two hours' drive, by which time he had almost reached Le Cateau, he was down to just one panzer battalion. The time had come to halt and find out what had happened to the rest of the division. Leaving the tanks in a position of all-round defense on a hill, Rommel, escorted by one tank, began to retrace his steps. He passed groups of French troops in bivouac but found only one of his infantry companies. He then spotted a French truck convoy. He pointed his pistol at the lead driver and ordered him to change direction and make for Avesnes, with Rommel acting as traffic policeman to ensure that the rest of the column followed him. Once they arrived in Avesnes, they were disarmed. It was now about 4:00 P.M., and the rest of the 7th Panzer Division began to arrive in Avesnes. Working off the map, Rommel directed the various elements to positions westward of Le Cateau. At a cost of 94 killed and wounded Rommel's men had netted some 10,000 prisoners, some 100 tanks, and 27 guns. But there was no time to rejoice over these spoils.

At midnight Rommel received orders to advance to Cambrai, fifteen miles west-northwest of Le Cateau. The division was, however, in urgent need of resupply, especially the tanks.

The battalion east of Le Cateau had also had to face a French tank attack and was subjected to shelling. Furthermore, the French had reoccupied one of the villages behind it. This situation could be dealt with by the infantry, and so Rommel took one of his other tank battalions around the village and linked up with the forward battalion. Finally, at 3:00 P.M. on May 18, the advance resumed. The country was open and rolling, ideally suited to tanks, and they advanced again in extended order. By dusk they had reached north of Cambrai and sealed all roads into the town.

Hitler and the German high command was, however, becoming worried about the success of the panzer thrust. The deeper it penetrated, the more it invited counterattacks into its ever longer flanks. There was, too, concern over the increasing wear and tear on men and machines. For these reasons Rommel was now ordered to halt where he was and give his division at least two days' rest and recuperation. The same order had also been passed to Kleist. Guderian, however, disagreed so strongly that he threatened to resign there and then. Rommel was also aghast; to allow the enemy breathing space at this juncture would undo much of what had been achieved. Victory was within the German grasp, and nothing should be spared to gain it as soon as possible. Their objections were listened to, and on the evening of the eighteenth Hitler relented and agreed that the advance could continue. Hoth's next objective was to be Arras, while Reinhardt and Guderian to the south were to make a wider sweep, with the English Channel as their objective, so as to totally cut off the northern Allied armies. Indeed, Guderian's tanks reached the mouth of the River Somme before the close of May 20. Hoth visited Rommel on the afternoon of May 19 and was told that Rommel intended to resume his advance that night. He queried whether the division had had enough rest. Rommel retorted that it had been in the same place for twenty hours and that an advance by night would save casualties. Hoth saw the sense in this and relented.

The 7th Panzer Division set off once more at 1:40 A.M. on May 20. Rommel was to swing round the south of Arras while the 5th Panzer Division to his north would move east of the town. It would thus be cut off. Thereafter they were to head for Bethune. Arras was held by the British with lightly armed troops, but to the north there were two infantry divisions. By daylight of the next day Rommel's advance had reached south of Arras. As usual he was with his panzer regiment, but he became irritated once more by the failure of his infantry to keep up, especially as its lagging enabled enemy forces to fill the resultant gap. It took a considerable time to sort this out, and then only after an additional infantry regiment and artillery had been deployed. He had received reports of strong British forces north of the city and so got this additional regiment to dig in. He then took his 6th Rifle Regiment and led it to join the tanks at the village of Wailly, four miles southwest of Arras. Just before he got there he became aware of one of his artillery batteries firing on tanks advancing from the north.

What had in fact happened was that the British, perceiving the growing threat to Arras, had decided to launch a counterattack. While on paper Lord Gort, the British commander, had two infantry divisions available as part of his reserve, they were depleted and had been partially committed to the defense of Arras itself. In terms of armor he only had the 1st Army Tank Brigade available. It consisted of slow-moving infantry support tanks, the majority armed with just machine guns. Only the sixteen heavily armored Matildas, armed with a two-pounder gun, were likely to have any effect on the situation, and it was these that the German guns had begun to engage.

Ensuring that his antitank guns were deployed, Rommel then moved into Wailly itself, where he found his own troops confused by the British tank fire. He restored order of sorts and then jumped into his armored car and drove up onto some high ground. From there he could see that one group of tanks was advancing from the west and another from the northwest. He returned to the antitank guns and succeeded in halting the British tanks. His own armor had already begun to move north, and Rommel now directed it to attack the British tanks in the flank. The British gave as good as they got, losing seven Matildas, but knocking out nine PzKwIIIs and IVs and a number of the lighter IIs. It was the end of the British attack, but on German side the reverberations would be felt at the very highest level.

It is true that the 7th Panzer Division suffered almost 400 casualties, including Rommel's aide-de-camp, killed beside him. The motorized SS Totenkopf (Death's Head), which was operating on Rommel's left flank and, because of its relative inexperience, was considerably more unsettled by the attack than Rommel's men, suffering a further 100 killed and wounded. Even though the British had a mere two tank battalions and two of infantry, their attack had been pressed home with greater determination than anything the Germans had so far experienced. It made Rundstedt halt the advance of his army group until the situation was cleared up, and he later called it the most critical moment of the whole campaign.[5] It would have been much more serious, however, if Rommel had not personally taken control of the situation. As it was, Rundstedt received fresh orders late on May 22 to squeeze the Allied pocket by advancing his armor to a line Armentières-Ypres-Ostend and by the infantry providing a shoulder on the high ground between Lens and St. Omer. Even so, Kleist remained nervous as a result of Arras, and the advance of his panzer group was more cautious as it moved up the coast than it had been. There was, too, renewed concern over the increasing number of tanks succumbing to mechanical breakdown. This all reached the ears of Hitler, and he decided that the armor must be halted. It needed to be conserved for Case Red, the plan for overrunning of the remainder of France. Thus on May 24 the panzers were ordered to halt, and Bock took the lead in reducing the now shrinking Allied pocket.

Rommel had spent May 22 and 23 edging his way round the west side of Arras, fully expecting another attack on his flank. The British then withdrew to the so-called Canal Line, which ran along the Bassée Canal to the sea. The 7th Panzer Division therefore came to rest in the Cuinchy area on the south side of the canal. On May 26 Hitler rescinded the halt order and on the same day the British set in motion the operation to evacuate the BEF from the beaches around Dunkirk. For Rommel the day meant renewed honors. He had already been awarded the 1939 Iron Cross Second and First Class for the Meuse crossings. Now he received the Knight's Cross of the Iron Cross, the first divisional commander of the campaign so honored.

There was no time to celebrate, for that night the 7th Rifle Brigade managed to establish a bridgehead on the north bank of the canal. Rommel went up to see for himself early next morning and found the bridgehead was too shallow. Furthermore, no heavy weapons had made it across and British snipers were very active. As so often before, Rommel took control of the situation. He organized suppressive fire against the snipers and ordered the construction of a bridge strong enough for tanks. Such was his progress that Hoth transferred the four tank battalions of the 5th Panzer Brigade from the 5th Panzer Division to his command. Rommel now advanced toward Lille, where there were sizable French forces. By the evening of May 27 his panzer battalions were closing on Lille, though widely dispersed. He gave orders to Rothenburg to establish a blocking position that night at Lomme on the northwest outskirts of the town, a move that would cut the one remaining westward escape route open to the French. This time Rommel did not accompany his tanks. Remembering how they had become isolated in front of Le Cateau, he decided that he would be better employed ensuring that the remainder of the division followed up and that supplies got through to Rothenberg. The 25th Panzer Regiment duly established its block in the early hours on the twenty-eighth and Rommel immediately set out to join it with a supply column and his reconnaissance battalion. The French did make a number of determined attempts to break out of Lille, but without success. During this contest Rommel had another narrow escape when a shell landed close to his signals vehicle, killed the commander of the reconnaissance battalion, and wounded several others. It turned out to have been fired by a German gun in a neighboring division.

On May 28 the Belgians surrendered. The evacuation from Dunkirk was now in full swing in spite of the efforts of the Luftwaffe to interdict it. The following day the 7th Panzer Division was withdrawn from the line to rest and refit. Then, on June 2, Hitler visited the division. Rommel wrote to Lucie that it was "wonderful. He greeted me with the words 'Rommel, we were very worried about you during the attack.'"[6] Rommel was then invited to accompany Hitler for the rest of the day. The latter made frequent reference to the Ghost Division, as the 7th Panzer was now being called because it had proved so elusive. Some of Rommel's fellow generals were jealous of his closeness to Hitler and they also disapproved of his relish at being in the limelight, but he was impervious to all this.

German troops entered Dunkirk on June 4. The evacuation was now over, and attention turned to the conquest of the rest of France. The 7th Panzer Division ended its rest on the same day and moved down to the Somme. There had been a major reorganization of forces. Rundstedt's Army Group A was now to cross the River Aisne and advance due south, while on his right Bock was to tackle the Somme and thrust southwestward, and seize the remaining French channel ports and overrun Brittany. To do this he was given three panzer corps, including that of Hoth. Rommel's mission was to cross the Somme Canal near Hangest, which lies between Amiens and Abbeville. The French had learned some lessons and laid out their defenses in much more depth than hitherto, but Rommel noted that a railway and a road bridge crossed the canal and hoped to capture them intact. His assault on June 5 was preceded by an impressive artillery bombardment, and, sure enough, his riflemen managed to capture the bridges before they could be blown. Rommel was soon there to see for himself and crossed on foot, leaving orders with the crew of his signals vehicle that it was to be the first across. His engineers hurriedly began to remove the rails from the railway bridge, and soon the 25th Panzer Regiment began to cross. A tank then shed its track on one bridge, blocking it for half an hour, but enough were across to start dealing with the French strongpoints. Recognizing that the French were standing and fighting, Rommel drew up a plan for a deliberate attack to break through their positions. The key point was the village of Quesnoy. Rommel arranged for his armor to move round the village from the north and subject it to intensive fire. It would then be cleared by the 7th Rifle Regiment. The attack was mounted at 4:00 P.M. and went according to plan in spite of stiff French resistance. The 7th Panzer Division began its breakout, but was ordered to halt because dive-bombers were about to clear the way ahead.

Next day 7th Panzer Division began its exploitation. Since the terrain was open, Rommel adopted a boxlike formation on a frontage of some 2,000 yards, but stretching back some twelve miles. The advantage of this formation was that the division could quickly concentrate on any point to meet any significant threat. During the next two days it advanced some thirty miles, eventually reaching the River Seine. Rommel's plan was to make a feint toward Rouen while he secured the bridge over the river at Elbreuf, which lay on the next river loop to the south. Matters did not turn out as he had hoped, however. The diversionary force, consisting of a tank company, field guns, and 88mm antiaircraft guns (now being used in the antitank role), ran across elements of the British 1st Armored Division, which was under French command after landing in France too late to join the BEF. These troops slowed his progress. Meanwhile Rommel, with the rest of his tanks, was trying to get to the south of Rouen. Night fell, and in the closeness of the Seine Valley radio communications became difficult. He had sent his motorcycle battalion to capture the Elbreuf bridge, but had no idea as to its progress. Concerned that his command might well be exposed to French artillery fire come dawn, Rommel went to Elbreuf and found chaos. French troops and civilians were clogging the town and trying to get across the river, and the motorcycle battalion commander had not been able to cope. Rommel, as usual, sorted out the situation, but just as he got the attack moving, the bridge blew up. Thus, he failed to get across the Seine, but then received new orders.

North of Rouen there was another stray British division, the 51st Highland, which had been helping to man the Maginot Line when the Germans attacked on May 10. It had just two brigades, since the third had been detached at the time and had fought with the main body of the BEF. Now it was withdrawing to the coast, together with French troops, hoping to reach the port of Le Havre so that it could be taken back to England. Rommel was therefore ordered to prevent this from happening. He acted immediately. He sent his reconnaissance battalion northward toward the coast and followed it up with the tanks. En route they clashed with groups of French troops withdrawing from the Somme. Rommel therefore formed a flank guard of antitank guns and pressed on, reaching the coast some ten miles west of St. Valéry-en-Caux, which the Highlanders had also reached. Rommel turned toward it, following behind three tanks. A French antitank gun knocked out the lead panzer and, to avoid a similar fate, the other two immediately fled the road without returning fire. Their flight exposed Rommel's own vehicle. The French gun fired at it a few times but missed. Rommel dismounted and got the two undamaged tanks to engage the gun and silence it. The two cowardly tank crews then felt the heat of his anger. However tired they might have been, there was no excuse for forgetting basic drills. Rommel then moved on to St. Valéry. The Scottish troops were determined to hold out in the hopes that friendly ships would arrive. It was not to be. The French troops in the town began to surrender, and General Victor Fortune, commanding the 51st Highland Division, was left with no option but to do the same. It was June 12 and Rommel personally took his surrender and that of the French corps commander.

Meanwhile, the Seine had been crossed, and the advance was moving toward the Loire. Rommel was ordered to capture the great port of Cherbourg at the top of the Cotentin Peninsula. He set off on July 17 and covered 150 miles in just twenty-four hours, meeting little resistance from a now rapidly disintegrating French army. By nightfall the following day his division was in position to capture the port. Rommel grabbed

June 17?

a few hours' sleep and the next day began his assault. After engaging the forts with artillery fire, Rommel demanded the port's surrender. When this was not forthcoming, Stukas attacked the docks and then Rommel's infantry went in. At 5:00 P.M. Cherbourg surrendered.

That was the end of Rommel's part in the 1940 French campaign. The exploits of the Ghost Division had demonstrated that the former infantryman had become an armored commander par excellence. His drive and determination had not diminished and neither had his personal courage. He had shown time and again the value of a commander being forward to maintain the momentum of the advance, thus ensuring that he retained the initiative, preventing timely reaction on the part of his opponents. He was indeed a man of the moment, but further challenges lay ahead.

CHAPTER 3

Libyan Sands

ON JUNE 25 THE HOSTILITIES CAME TO AN END WHEN France signed an armistice in the very same railway coach in which the Germans had signed the armistice that ended World War I in November 1918. Rommel, like all other Germans who had fought in the campaign, was tired but euphoric. With France defeated, few believed that Britain would hold out on its own, and there was a feeling that Europe would soon be at peace again, with Germany dominant. Rommel himself was beginning to become a household name in Germany. Joseph Goebbels was keen to make use of him for propaganda purposes, and Hitler asked especially for Rommel to send him a map charting his division's progress across Belgium and France. There is no doubt that Rommel had performed

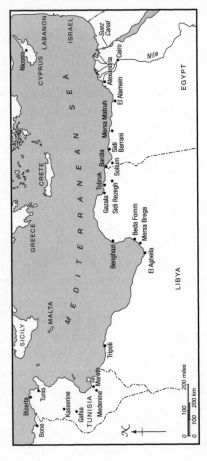

North Africa 1941–1943. Map by David Hoxley.

brilliantly in the campaign, and he knew it. He welcomed Hitler's continued personal interest in him and thoroughly enjoyed the adulation and publicity he was receiving, much in the way General Norman Schwarzkopf did after the successes of the 1991 Gulf War. Yet not all thought Rommel perfect. His superior officer during the campaign, Hermann Hoth, commented in a confidential report he made in July 1940 that Rommel was too impulsive and needed to gain "greater experience and a better sense of judgement" to qualify for command of a corps. Hoth also accused Rommel of not recognizing the contribution made by others in his battles.[1] The officers of the 5th Panzer Division, his sister formation in the XV Panzer Corps, were apparently especially bitter. They resented that twice during the campaign elements of their division had been placed under Rommel's command and he had shown no gratitude.

The 7th Panzer Division remained in northern France. Initially it was a period of refitting and a chance for its men to go home on leave. Frustrated by Britain's refusal to come to terms, Hitler resolved that it had to be crushed and began to make preparations for an invasion. To succeed he needed to gain supremacy in the air over southern England and so launched a sustained offensive that began in earnest in mid-August. While this, the Battle of Britain, was being fought, Rommel underwent a novel experience. Goebbels asked for his help in making a film on the French campaign titled *Triumph in the West*. In particular, Goebbels wanted to show the Ghost Division's crossing of the River Somme, and so Rommel was asked to recreate it. This he did, with the help of French colonial prisoners of war who played the part of the defenders of Le Quesnoy. The filming seems to have been an enjoyable experience and he was pleased with the final result.

The Luftwaffe, failing in its mission to destroy the Royal Air Force, resorted instead to the bombing of Britain's cities, and Hitler turned his eyes eastward, toward the Soviet Union. Rommel's division was transferred to Bordeaux. He went home to Wiener Neustadt for Christmas leave, but it was cut short by the scare of a possible revolt in unoccupied France. Should it have occurred, Germans forces, including the 7th Panzer Division, would have had to move in, and so he spent Christmas on standby. He did, however, receive one present that pleased him. He had sent Hitler a meticulously prepared diary of his division's exploits and received a letter of thanks just before Christmas. "You can be proud of your achievements," Hitler wrote.[2]

At the beginning of February 1941, Rommel was able to resume his interrupted leave in Wiener Neustadt. Once again, though, he had to end it hurriedly. One of Hitler's adjutants arrived at his door with an urgent message. Rommel was to go to Berlin and report to Field Marshal Walther von Brauchitsch, the army's commander in chief, and then to Hitler. He flew to Berlin the next day, February 6, and saw Brauchitsch in the morning and Hitler after lunch. He was informed that he was to command a German contingent of two divisions, the 5th Light and the 21st Panzer, which were being sent to Libya to assist the Italians. Besides giving Rommel the opportunity to practice his skills in an entirely new environment, the desert, the appointment was significant in other ways. German ground forces at the time were not actively engaged in any theater of war, and the choice of Rommel, in addition to being a signal honor to him personally, conveyed to the world that Germany was standing by its ally and sending its best ambassador to the Italians, impressing them and encouraging them to fight harder against the British.

Italy had finally entered the war on the German side just before the fall of France in June 1940 and mounted an attack on the south of that country before agreeing to the armistice. Mussolini, however, was more interested in enlarging his African empire at the expense of the British. In mid-August his troops invaded and quickly overran British Somaliland (present-day Somalia) and also made incursions into Sudan, but Egypt was the greatest prize, and he gave orders for his troops in neighboring Libya to attack it the day Germany invaded Britain. Of course, that invasion never happened, but the Italian operation went ahead. On September 13 five divisions, with 200 tanks, crossed the border, advanced sixty miles in three days, and then, nervous of advancing any farther, consolidated by constructing a series of fortified camps. The British, having numerically inferior forces, did little to oppose this advance, but during the next few months carried out a number of raids on the Italian camps. Then, on December 9, they struck, using the open desert to outflank the Italian camps, taking them totally by surprise, and driving the Italian forces out of Egypt, and into Libya. The port of Tobruk fell on January 22, and the Italian Tenth Army withdrew along the coast road toward Benghazi. To cut it off, British armor traversed the difficult terrain south of the semi-mountainous Jebel Akhdar, established a blocking position on the road running south from Benghazi, and fought a battle there during February 6–7. Twenty thousand Italians, 200 guns, and 120 tanks fell into British hands. The remaining Italian forces retreated from Cyrenaica and into the neighboring province of Tripolitania. The Italians had also suffered badly at the hands of the Greeks when they attempted to invade that country from Albania, and it became clear in Hitler's mind that he had to do something to prop up his ally. Hence his decision, made even before the British victory at

Beda Fomm south of Benghazi, to send Rommel to Libya. Indeed, as early as January 11 he had issued a directive to reinforce Libya under the code name Sunflower.

Rommel wrote to Lucie as soon as he had been briefed: "I need not tell you how my head is swimming with all the many things there are to be done. . . . So 'our leave' was cut short again. Don't be sad, it had to be. The new job is very big and important." Next day he gave Lucie a hint as to where he was going, writing that it would be a way of getting a cure for his rheumatism: he had been advised to go to Egypt. She was thus able to put two and two together.[3] He flew first to Rome. There, on February 11, he reported to the deputy chief of staff of the Italian high command (*Commando Supremo*), General Alfredo Guzzoni, who told him the bad news of the defeat at Beda Fomm. Rommel had already drawn up a plan for defending Tripolitania, and it was approved. It was arranged that General Mario Roatta, the Italian army chief of staff, would join him in Libya. Rommel then flew there via Sicily, where elements of the Luftwaffe had already been deployed. He asked their commander to bomb Benghazi to prevent the British from using its port for supplies and thus impede any British advance into Tripoli. The airman stated that the Italians would not be happy since a number of their officers and officials owned properties there. Rommel then contacted Hitler's headquarters and received clearance. The bombing went ahead, but the whole incident indicated that he might find dealing with his allies frustrating.

Arriving in Tripoli the next day, February 12, Rommel was told that Marshal Rodolfo Graziani, the commander in chief of Italian North Africa, had just resigned and had been replaced by his chief of staff, General Italo Gariboldi, whom Rommel had just met. He tried to impress on the Italian the importance of establishing a forward defense in Tripolitania in the area of the Gulf of Sirte. Gariboldi, still in shock after the recent reverse, was dubious and advised Rommel to look at the terrain for himself. Without hesitation Rommel organized a plane and flew over the area. His excursion confirmed what his map study en route to Libya had shown him, and he told Gariboldi so that evening. Roatta had now arrived with a directive from Mussolini that Rommel's plan was to be put into operation, and there were no further objections. It was arranged that two Italian infantry divisions would move up from the Tripoli area the next day, followed by the Ariete Division, a motorized formation with some tanks. It was, however, going to take time to deploy this force, given that it was faced with a 250-mile march and there was insufficient transport to lift both infantry divisions at once. Should the British attack in the meantime, all that could hold them up was the Luftwaffe.

Rommel's fears were proved largely groundless. The British forces in Cyrenaica, especially the British tanks, had suffered considerable wear and tear during their recent successful campaign. Their crack 7th Armored Division and 6th Australian Division had to be sent back to Egypt to be reequipped. The former was replaced by the 2nd Armored Division, which was newly arrived in North Africa and had to be partially equipped for the desert with captured Italian tanks. The situation was further aggravated by Winston Churchill's decision on February 23 to send forces that included one of 2nd Armored's brigades to help the Greeks, who had been fighting an Italian invasion from Albania since the previous November. Thus, the British did not have the resources to advance farther.

On February 14 the first elements of the Deutsches Afrika Korps (DAK), the reconnaissance and antitank battalions of the 5th Light Division, arrived in Tripoli Harbor. They were given little time to find their bearings. Once they had been issued their tropical uniforms and paraded before the Italian high command, Rommel sent them up to Sirte. On February 24 Rommel ordered his reconnaissance battalion to probe forward and make contact with the enemy so as to give the impression of joint Italian and German activity. The probe surprised a British armored car patrol, and an officer and two soldiers were taken prisoner. During the next couple of weeks it began to dawn on Rommel and his intelligence staff that the British were weaker than was thought and were unlikely to attack. In the meantime the rest of the 5th Light Division was arriving, including, on March 11, its most important element in Rommel's eyes, the 5th Panzer Regiment: 120 tanks, half of them PzKw IIIs and IVs and the remainder light tanks. It was now that Rommel moved up into the desert himself, establishing his headquarters at Sirte. Then, on March 19, he flew to Berlin. Before he did so he left orders with the 5th Light Division to prepare for an attack on the forward British position at El Agheila.

Rommel was decorated with Oak Leaves to his Knight's Cross while in Berlin. The award was further, albeit much delayed, recognition of his achievements in France. Otherwise the visit left a sour taste in his mouth. Brauchitsch told him that to go on the offensive was not in the cards and that he could not expect the 15th Panzer Division, the other major element of the DAK, to arrive until the end of May. When it did, he could advance as far as Agedabia, and possibly to Benghazi, but that was all; he should bear in mind that his mission was the defense of Tripolitania. Rommel held his tongue, apart from pointing out that such an operation would merely leave his flank exposed and that he would have to advance to the other side of the Cyrenaica "bulge," encompassing the Jebel Akhdar to secure his position. On his return to Africa the 3rd

Reconnaissance Battalion duly mounted the attack on El Agheila and captured the fort and airfield. The British hurriedly withdrew to Mersa Brega. There was a defile here, and Rommel reasoned that it would be both a good place to launch the Agedabia attack and an excellent defensive position. He attacked on March 31. This time the British did resist, but Rommel found a route through the sand hills north of the coast road and was able to outflank them. By evening the gorge and eighty British vehicles were in his hands. The next day, air reconnaissance and patrols sent out by General Johannes Streich, commander of the 5th Light Division, indicated that the British were withdrawing. Sir Archibald Wavell, the British commander in chief in the Middle East, had given orders to the Western Desert Force in Cyrenaica that its task was not to hold ground, but to delay the enemy, keeping its own force intact until reinforcements arrived.

To Rommel the opportunity was too good to miss, even if it meant disobeying the orders that Berlin had given him. His plan was to seize Agedabia and then divide his force in two. While one part was to advance directly to Benghazi, the other, with part of the 5th Light Division and an Italian reconnaissance battalion, was to strike across the base of the Cyrenaica bulge and head for Derna, thus cutting the escape route via the coast road from Benghazi. It was a mirror image of a tactic employed by the British two months earlier. There was one difference, though. Between the two groups the 5th Panzer Regiment was to head for Msus and then Mechili, thus blocking other avenues of escape.

The operation began on April 2. Agedabia fell that afternoon, and by evening the British had been driven twelve miles to the east. The next day Rommel moved his headquarters to Agedabia, and the pursuit began in earnest as it became clear that the British intended to abandon Cyrenaica. Yet not all were happy. In particular, Streich had his doubts. He had commanded a regiment in the 5th Panzer Division in France and had formed an unfavorable opinion of Rommel, considering him to be a self-centered opportunist. Now he expressed concerns over the state of some of his vehicles. Rommel dismissed them. "One cannot permit unique opportunities to slip for the sake of trifles," he commented.[4] Later that day Streich stated that they would have to halt for four days to replenish their vehicles. Rommel immediately ordered the division to unload all its trucks, send them back to the divisional supply point, and return with sufficient fuel, ammunition, and rations to sustain the division for an advance to the Egyptian border. He gave them just twenty-four hours to do this. That evening he had a visit from Gariboldi, who expressed his displeasure in no uncertain terms, stating that Rommel's actions were a flagrant breach of his orders from Rome and adding that the precarious supply situation did not allow for the advance. Rommel was to call off the action and told not make any further moves without Gariboldi's permission. Rommel dug his toes in, declaring that he would continue to advance whatever the consequences. At that moment a signal arrived from the German high command giving Rommel a free hand. There was nothing more to be said.

On the night of April 3 German reconnaissance elements entered Benghazi, which had been hurriedly evacuated by the British. The advance got into full swing. Rommel spent much of the time in the air. He had frequently used a Fieseler Storch light aircraft in France, and here in the desert he found it an ideal means of keeping his finger on the pulse of the action. If he thought a column was moving too slowly, he would drop a message telling it so and warning that he would land if it did not speed up. The British confusion grew as their forces retreated eastward. Some of the armor ran out of fuel and tanks were abandoned. On April 5 Rommel received reports that Mechili was cleared of the enemy. He ordered the 5th Panzer Regiment to press on and secure it. Later he was told that in fact Mechili was strongly held. He therefore joined the remainder of the 5th Light Division on the right, intending to bypass Mechili and push on to the coast road. Rough terrain and fuel shortages served to delay matters. At one point Rommel himself personally took charge of scavenging fuel so that the Italian artillery could be deployed for the Mechili attack. There was, however, no sign of the panzers. Rommel spent much of April 7 in his Storch searching for them. Just as the light was fading he located them well north of their planned route. He landed in a vile mood and told Colonel Herbert Olbrich to advance at best speed during the night to the east of Mechili. He then took off again to return to his headquarters in the darkness. The next day, all finally fell into place. The right had assaulted Mechili, and Rommel, airborne again, saw its defenders withdrawing westward. Then the 5th Panzer Regiment appeared and the number of prisoners increased. Meanwhile reconnaissance elements had reached the coast road, and Rommel sent them reinforcements and arrived at Derna himself that evening. In a week he had driven the British pell-mell out of the Cyrenaica bulge and so could be reasonably expected to be satisfied and pause so that his men could draw breath. But that was not Rommel's style. It was the same drive in the face of growing fatigue that enabled the Allies to liberate Kuwait in the shortest possible time in 1991 and to thrust without halt to Baghdad in 2003.

On April 9 Rommel returned to Mechili and found the 5th Light Division beginning a two-day halt to replenish and carry out much needed maintenance on its vehicles. Rommel told Streich that his break was canceled. Instead he was to be at Gazala by dawn next day in readiness for an attack on Tobruk.

Rommel's ultimate goal was the Suez Canal. With ever lengthening supply lines it was essential that the port of Tobruk be brought into operation, especially since it was the only one of note west of Alexandria. Hence this port was to be his next objective. But the British also recognized the importance of Tobruk. On April 6 Wavell had laid down that it must be turned into a fortress, a demand echoed by Winston Churchill in a signal the next day. Both General Philip Neame, the commander of the Western Desert Force, and General Dick O'Connor, victor of the first desert campaign, who had been sent to advise Neame, had been captured, and so Wavell flew up to Tobruk to organize its defense. This was based on General Owen Morshead's 9th Australian Division and contained the equivalent of six infantry brigades supported by four field artillery regiments (battalions in U.S. terms), antiguns, antiaircraft artillery, and forty-five tanks. The tank strength was boosted by reinforcements Wavell sent by sea. The Axis forces could therefore expect a stiff fight, but Rommel did not appreciate that at the time.

Rommel's plan was to quickly envelop the port and then attack from several directions. The Italian Brescia and Trento Divisions were to demonstrate in the west, while the 5th Light Division carried out the envelopment. The Ariete Division was to deploy to El Adem, south of Tobruk, and be prepared to help the 5th Light Division. The envelopment was completed on April 11, and preparations were made for the actual assault on the defenses. Streich, who had been entrusted with this mission, was unhappy again, this time over the lack of intelligence about the Tobruk defenses. Nevertheless, the attack went ahead in the afternoon of the next day. The Brescia Division attacked first as a feint; the 5th Panzer Regiment attacked from the south but was brought to a halt by an antitank ditch. Rommel accepted that the attack had failed and next day sent in the 3rd Reconnaissance Battalion to destroy the antitank ditch. The battalion managed to break into the defenses and established a lodgment, but it was unclear whether the antitank ditch had been neutralized. The 5th Light Division's attack was scheduled for 12:30 A.M. on April 13. Rommel decided it should proceed since the lodgment made would be a good jump-off position.

The initial reports on the attack were promising, and so Rommel set off to get the Ariete in motion to follow up. He returned to his headquarters at 9:00 A.M. to learn that the attack had ground to a halt because the frontage was too narrow. It turned out that the 5th Light Division had come under intense fire, and Olbrich had been forced to withdraw his tanks. Rommel was furious that the attacking infantry had thus been left in the lurch. He ordered the tanks to go back in. He then went to harass the Ariete. Returning to the 5th Light Division, he found that nothing had been done because of the intense British fire. He therefore felt forced to call off the attack. To cap off a bad day, he returned once more to bring the Ariete up into a position next to the 5th Light Division. As they moved up, they came under artillery fire, which apparently scattered them.

Rommel's attempt to take Tobruk had failed. He recognized that the lack of intelligence was the main cause, although he blamed much of it on the Italians, who had failed to give him the plans of the defenses they had previously constructed. He decided therefore to pause before making another attempt and turned his attention to the situation on the frontier. This pause did not mean that Tobruk went quiet. Both sides made a number of local attacks, and Rommel became aware that his besieging force was stretched thin. He did, however, finally receive a copy of the Italian plan of the defenses, which enabled him to begin planning his next major assault, which would take place at the end of April or early May.

He had sent a battalion to capture Bardia, the last town on the road to the Egyptian frontier, while he invested Tobruk. Rommel visited the unit on April 19, decorating its commander with the Knight's Cross and ordering him to occupy the fortress there with a company. On the way back his small group of vehicles was attacked by British aircraft. The driver of his cross-country vehicle was killed, as was his motorcycle dispatch rider. His Mammoth, a command vehicle captured from the British, also suffered, its driver wounded. Leaving his aide with the damaged vehicles, Rommel took the wheel of the Mammoth, which was still roadworthy, and tried to make his way back to his headquarters by taking a shortcut across the desert. Night had fallen and he tried to navigate by the stars, but clouds then came over. He was forced to halt until daylight. It was another narrow escape and yet another example of a commander who was consistently prepared to roll up his sleeves and get his hands dirty.

On April 25 his men crossed the Egyptian frontier and captured the Halfaya Pass through which the coast road ran and Sollum just to its north. The British fell back to the line Buq Buq–Sofafi and began to construct a fallback defensive position at Mersa Matruh, a hundred miles farther east.

Rommel now concentrated on preparing for the second major assault on Tobruk. Before it could take place he was visited by General Friedrich Paulus, chief of the Operations Branch of the Oberkommando des Heeres (OKH), the German army headquarters, and a contemporary of Rommel. His mission was to check up on exactly how the DAK commander had achieved his success, which OKH mistakenly believed had also brought about the British withdrawal from Greece. Paulus had stated that the plan had been to keep the British trapped there, to which Rommel retorted that no one had informed him of this. Indeed, he considered the German attack on Yugoslavia and Greece earlier in April as a mistaken use of force and felt the troops involved would have been much better employed in North Africa, where they could have been used to deny the British the Mediterranean. This, of course, reveals that Rommel clearly had no idea of the reason for the Balkans invasion, namely, to secure the German southern flank for the impending invasion of Russia. Paulus also wanted to know what Rommel planned to do next. He had the power to okay it or veto it on the spot, especially if Rommel intended to advance to the Suez Canal, which he did. In this context Paulus sanctioned the next attack on Tobruk, which took place on April 30. It was, however, more limited than Rommel had originally intended and was aimed at capturing a key feature on the western side of the perimeter. It was successful, but at a price of over 1,200 casualties, and Paulus was not particularly impressed. He was also concerned over the logistics situation. The extended supply lines meant that the troops were suffering hardships and Paulus felt it better if Rommel withdrew his forces to Gazala in order to shorten them. Rommel, who was sharing the same rations as his men and seemed as impervious to hardship as he had been as a young man, disagreed. Rather, he stated, the Italians should make more effort to develop the port of Benghazi so that the DAK could be supplied from there. Paulus pointed out that the cross-Mediterranean route to Benghazi was longer than that to Tripoli, exposing it even more to British naval attack, and that Tripoli's capacity was much greater. He also made it plain to Rommel that he could expect no further reinforcements and had to remain on the defensive after taking Tobruk.

When Paulus left, Rommel turned his attention once more to the Egyptian frontier. His intelligence told him that the British might be preparing an attack, since their radios had fallen silent. Even so, when the British attacked on May 15 they surprised the Germans, drove Rommel's men out of the Halfaya Pass, and recaptured Sollum and Capuzzo. Rommel reacted quickly, sending forward a panzer battalion, with some 88mm antitank guns, to drive the British back, apart from Halfaya Pass, to which the British continued to cling. It was during this action that the Germans employed a new tactic with their antitank guns. They used their tanks as bait to draw the British armor on, while screening their own antitank guns. The Panzers would then move to the flanks, leaving the British tanks exposed. Rommel also now employed battle groups to an increasing extent. These were ad hoc all-arms groupings tailored to a particular situation and named after their commanders. Their use reflected his increased confidence in the troops under his command, which had previously been lacking to a degree simply because Rommel had had no opportunity to train them in his methods before battle was joined. He used the battle groups to good effect at the end of May when he recaptured Halfaya Pass.

During this time Rommel got into hot water with OKH. The supply situation remained problematic, especially since the British were enjoying some success against supply vessels crossing the Mediterranean. In an effort to increase the rate of resupply Rommel resorted to exaggerating his reports to OKH on his shortages. Brauchitsch took umbrage and sent Rommel a stern rebuke, but it appears to have made little difference. As he wrote to Lucie: "I am not going to take it lying down, and a letter is already on its way to v. B."[5]

By now the Egyptian summer was in full force and Rommel recorded a temperature of 107 degrees Fahrenheit on June 2.

It was, however, a dry heat and did not act as a brake on operations. Indeed, on June 15 the British mounted another attack code-named Battleaxe. It was much more ambitious than their attack the previous month and aimed at nothing less than the relief of Tobruk and then exploitation to Derna and Mechili. Rommel's radio interception service had picked up the code word "Peter" the previous day. Suspecting an attack, Rommel put his troops on maximum alert. He also deployed antitank guns in good fire positions, and the 5th Light Division (Rommel had removed Streich from command of the division, telling him that he cared too much for the welfare of his men. His successor was Johannes von Ravenstein, another Pour le Mérite winner) and 15th Panzer Division, now finally complete in-theater, were on standby to move forward from Tobruk. There was a fuel shortage, and Rommel did not want to commit them until he knew precisely the direction of the attack. When it came early on the fifteenth it was two-pronged, with the 4th Indian Division, supported by infantry tanks and an armored brigade from the 7th Armored Division; they attacked Halfaya Pass, Sollum, and Capuzzo, while the remainder of the 7th in the south was headed for Bardia. Capuzzo fell, but, largely thanks to the antitank guns, the rest of the defenses stood up well. Rommel was hence able to conserve most of his mobile reserve, although the 15th Panzer Division's panzer regiment was committed to the area of Capuzzo and lost some tanks. The coming of night caused a pause and enabled Rommel to plan for the next day. He intended to use the 15th Panzer Division to attack both British prongs frontally and pin them down while the 5th Light Division would go round to the south and then turn north toward Halfaya Pass and thus cut the British off. The second day of the action was marked by fierce tank battles, but by the end of it Rommel sensed, again largely thanks to radio intercepts, that his enemy was weakening. Accordingly, he ordered the 15th Panzer Division to disengage and join the 5th Light Division for the decisive thrust north to Halfaya. This action began at dawn on June 17, but struck empty air. The British had suffered the loss of over ninety tanks and had withdrawn overnight.

Rommel was naturally elated by his victory. Certainly the German propaganda machine made the most of it, but Rommel's hopes that he might receive reinforcements and be allowed to pursue his dream of reaching the Suez Canal were soon dashed. On June 22, 1941, Hitler launched his invasion of the Soviet Union. At a stroke North Africa was reduced to a sideshow. Moreover, OKH clearly did not trust Rommel. General Franz Halder, its chief of staff, had noted on May 11, just after Paulus left North Africa, that "by overstepping his orders, Rommel has brought about a situation for which our present supply capabilities are insufficient. Rommel cannot cope with the situation."[6] The plan was hatched to place Rommel under the authority of a German headquarters so that he could be more easily controlled, but a week later Halder noted that Hitler did not want him "hampered" in this way. Halder's views were further reinforced by a talk that he had in early July with General Alfred Gause, the German OKH liaison officer to the Italian high command in North Africa. Gause said that he found it difficult to get along with Rommel because of the his character and "inordinate ambition." No one dared to oppose him because of "his brutality and backing he has on top level [i.e., Hitler]."[7] There was, on the other hand, a recognition that Rommel was actually commanding considerably more than a mere corps of two divisions. This was recognized on July 1 by his promotion to general of panzer troops. The following month his command was raised to that of Panzer Group. Directly under his command were two panzer divisions (the 5th

Light Division had now become the 21st Panzer Division) and a new formation, the 90th Light Division, which had been formed from German units in Africa that were not part of the panzer divisions. It consisted of three motorized regiments. Although it was not formally under his command, Rommel also had the use of the Italian XX Corps, with the Ariete and Trieste motorized divisions, the four infantry divisions of XXI Corps, and an additional Italian infantry division.

OKH organized a new staff under Gause to help run affairs. The idea was that it would act as a bridge between the Italian theater high command and OKH and would also be concerned with supply matters. It was announced to Rommel as a fait accompli, and he was understandably suspicious. The staff, however, was of high quality and fully accepted Rommel's demand that they were there primarily to assist him and not put obstacles in his way. The relationship was quickly cemented, and he was able to write to Lucie at the end of August that he was "getting on famously" with Gause.[8]

As for the overall situation, Tobruk was still firmly under siege, and Rommel intended to attack it again in the autumn, once he had built up his supplies. On the British side there had been a change of command. Wavell had been replaced by Sir Claude Auchinleck. He was charged by Churchill with relieving Tobruk, but refused to undertake the task until he was ready. In the meantime he built up his forces in what was now the Eighth Army. Rommel himself suffered from attacks of jaundice during the summer, luckily none of them for very long. There was also frustration that supplies and reinforcements were not reaching him at the desired rate, and he was forced to postpone his attack on Tobruk from September to November. At the beginning of that month he was, however, able to see Lucie again after an absence of nine months. The two were able to snatch a few days in Rome.

Rommel returned to Africa in mid-November. While in Rome he had briefed Marshal Ugo Cavallero, the head of the Italian supreme command, on his impending attack on To-bruk. When the marshal expressed concerns over a likely British offensive, Rommel dismissed them. He was confident that he could repel any attack, as he had done in the summer. He had improved his defenses on the frontier and had his two panzer divisions deployed for any eventuality. Indeed, he envisaged the 21th Panzer Division taking advantage of the open desert to strike any incursion in its flank. Furthermore, if he took Tobruk it would remove the reason for a British attack. As it happened, on November 18 the British struck first.

Strict radio silence and maneuvering by night prevented the Germans from detecting the attack before it happened. The plan called for XIII Corps, with the New Zealand Division and 4th Indian Division, with infantry tanks, to attack Sidi Omar and Capuzzo and then tackle Sollum and Bardia. Simultaneously XXX Corps, with the bulk of the armor, was to advance northwestward to a point some thirty miles south of Tobruk. The idea behind this was to draw the Axis armor into battle and destroy it. This done, Tobruk could be relieved. It took the Germans some hours to realize that a major offensive was under way. The British armor therefore advanced in three columns unhindered. Indeed, it was not until the next day that they came up against Rommel's screen. The left-hand column comprised the 22nd Armored Brigade and this struck the Ariete Division at Bir el Gubi and received a bloody nose. In the center the 7th Armored Brigade reached Sidi Rizegh, just five miles southeast of Tobruk, while the 22nd Armored Brigade on the left was itself attacked from the north by the 5th Panzer Regiment at Gabr Saleh. Ravenstein, anxious about the rapidly developing situation, had used his own initiative to make this move. A fierce tank battle then erupted, which lasted from the late afternoon until darkness fell, when both sides withdrew to rest for the night. At this stage Ludwig Crüwell, who had succeeded Rommel as commander of the DAK, had been uncharacteristically allowed a free hand by his superior, apart from a general order to destroy all enemy forces that had crossed the frontier. He was in the dark as much as anyone else as to what was happening, but Rommel still left him to his own devices.

On November 20 the 22nd Armored Brigade moved to join the 4th Armored Brigade at Gabr Saleh, while Crüwell ordered his panzer division to sweep southward. The 15th Panzer fought another action at Gabr Saleh and got the best of it, but the 21st Panzer Division ran out of fuel. That evening, Rommel stepped in. He had already ordered the 90th Light to establish a blocking position at Sidi Rizegh, and he now ordered Crüwell to move to the same place, recognizing that the 7th Armored Brigade and the motorized infantry of the 7th Armored Division posed the greatest threat to Tobruk, especially if the garrison tried to break out. This, indeed, was the British plan, and it was put into effect at dawn the next day. Rommel positioned himself there to conduct the battle, which resulted in the British being repulsed. By evening the DAK had arrived, and the danger had, for the moment, been averted.

The British now concentrated their armor for another attempt at Sidi Rizegh the next day. Crüwell was, though, worried by XIII Corps, which looked poised to advance along the coast toward Tobruk. Consequently, he wanted to move his panzer division eastward to meet this threat. Rommel, however, insisted that he leave the 21st Panzer Division at Belhamed, while the 15th Panzer Division moved to Gambut, eighteen miles away. While XIII Corps did begin to advance on Tobruk on November 22, the same day saw Rommel order the 21st Panzer Division to attack the British at Sidi Rizegh. This was successful. The 7th Armored Brigade and 7th Armored Division Support Group, which contained its infantry, suffered heavily and were forced to withdraw. Rommel sensed that the decisive phase of the battle had arrived. He ordered Crüwell to take the 15th Panzer Division and the tanks from the 21st Panzer Division on a drive southwest from east of Tobruk and link up with the Ariete, which had been ordered to move southeast. In this way he aimed to trap XXX Corps south of Sidi Rizegh. Crüwell set off at dawn on the twenty-third, but suffered an early setback when most of his DAK staff were captured by the New Zealand Division advancing toward Tobruk. Undeterred, he continued and soon ran across some supply columns of XXX Corps, which he scattered. The combined force then turned north, tanks leading, and inflicted severe damage on a South African brigade that was in its path. It in turn was hit by the remaining tanks of the 22nd Armored Brigade, which moved from west to east across the rear of Crüwell's advance. When the two sides withdrew at the end of the day, both had suffered heavily.

Rommel did not interfere at all with Crüwell's operations. He was much more concerned with Tobruk itself. While the 90th Light Division was preventing the garrison from a successful breakout, the progress of the New Zealanders preoccupied him. Nevertheless, that night he was pleased with the way the battle was unfolding, especially that Crüwell seemed to have achieved his aim of destroying the XXX Corps armor. The time had come to wrap up the whole affair. To this end, Rommel intended to take what remained of the DAK on a wide sweep south and west round the Eighth Army's southern flank and link up with the Bardia and Halfaya Pass garrisons, which were still holding out, and thus cut the British off. It was a typically bold Rommel maneuver against an enemy he sensed was already beaten, although with XIII Corps still advancing this was not quite the case.

What became known by the British as "the dash to the Wire"—the Wire being the popular name for the Egyptian-Libyan frontier—began at 10:30 A.M. on November 24. Rommel led the way with the 21st Panzer Division after having told his subordinate commanders to ignore anything happening on the flanks. For some reason he took Gause, whom he had now made his chief of staff, with him. This movement concerned his staff, especially with the New Zealanders approaching ever closer to Tobruk. There was also no clear indication of what had happened to XXX Corps, apart from the fact that it appeared scattered. There was also the question of how the DAK could be resupplied behind the enemy's front line. But there was nothing they could do about it.

As it was, Rommel's dash achieved little. Unbeknown to him, there were two forward supply dumps south of the track he took. If he had captured them, he would have solved his own supply problem and dealt a severe blow to the Eighth Army, but he missed them. He also ran across very little of XXX Corps and failed to relieve the frontier garrisons. The only success was the overrunning of a New Zealand brigade headquarters and the removal of Sir Alan Cunningham from command of the Eighth Army. The presence of Rommel panicked him, and he wanted to pull back across the frontier. Auchinleck held his nerve, removed Cunningham, and took over the Eighth Army himself. Meanwhile back at the Panzer Group Africa headquarters the staff had spent November 25 with a very anxious Italian commander in chief breathing over them as they watched the steady progress of the New Zealanders. They retook Sidi Rizegh in a skillful night attack. Elements of the Tobruk garrison broke out, and a narrow corridor was established to link them up with the New Zealanders.

Lieutenant Colonel Siegfried Westphal, the head of the operations branch at the headquarters, now used his own initiative. On November 26 he managed to contact the 21st Panzer Division and ordered them back to Tobruk. He informed Rommel by signal of what he had done, warning that the DAK could find itself stranded because of the resupply problems and that the British were now enjoying air superiority over the battlefield. Rommel finally relented the following day and returned with the DAK. It happened to be his wedding anniversary, and he wrote in a letter to Lucie: "I've just spent four days in a desert counterattack with nothing to wash with. We had a splendid success."[9] These were brave words. While he might have caused the Eighth Army some disruption, he had not reduced the growing crisis around Tobruk.

Rommel's immediate task was to remove the New Zealand Division from Sidi Rizegh and close the corridor to Tobruk. On the evening of the twenty-eighth, he summoned Crüwell to his forward headquarters, which was near Gambut. Crüwell had difficulty in finding it, but eventually came across a British truck. He approached it with understandable caution. Inside he discovered Rommel and Gause, unshaven, caked in desert sand, and clearly showing their lack of sleep. A heap of straw provided a bed, and there was a can of stale water and a few tins of food. Two wireless trucks and some dispatch riders constituted the rest of the headquarters. Rommel told Crüwell that he wanted him to surround the New Zealanders and destroy them. Crüwell's subsequent orders called for both panzer divisions to advance from the east, one north of Sidi Rizegh and the other to the south, but Rommel countermanded this on the grounds that it would merely drive the New Zealanders into Tobruk and so strengthen the garrison. Instead, the 15th Panzer Division was to turn north once it had passed Sidi Rizegh in the south and head for El Duda. The operation was largely successful. El Duda was captured, although it was then lost again, and the New Zealanders were all but surrounded and forced to withdraw. Yet the corridor to Tobruk remained open. Also, Ravenstein, the dashing commander of the 21st Panzer Division, had fallen into British hands.

The strain on the Axis forces, especially the mobile elements, was beginning to tell, and the supply situation was deteriorating. On December 1 Rommel's intelligence branch, largely thanks to radio intercepts, was able to construct a reasonably accurate British order of battle. It showed that the Eighth Army was still very much intact in spite of its losses. There may also have been the influence of a BBC news broadcast on the same day. It gave a brief but accurate account of the fighting over the past couple of days and went on to state: "The British troops are newly supplied and reinforced, whereas the German and Italian troops are laboring under serious supply difficulties."[10] Rommel began to realize that time was against him. Yet he was still determined to have one more attempt to relieve the frontier garrisons. It failed, and Rommel saw that he would have to relinquish his hold on the eastern part of the Tobruk perimeter. At the same time he received reports that the British were concentrating a force in the area of Bir el Gobi, south of Sidi Rizegh. The threat to the whole Tobruk perimeter was obvious if this force was able to outflank it. Consequently, on the night of December 4–5 the DAK was deployed to El Adem. It was supposed to launch an attack on Bir el Gobi in conjunction with the Italian XX Corps, but this corps was in no fit state to take part, and so the DAK went on its own. It had some success but failed to destroy the British force, which consisted of a newly arrived infantry brigade and two refitted armored brigades. Worse, the Tobruk garrison had attacked and seized the high ground running from El Duda to Belhamed. Rommel thus had no option but to withdraw his remaining forces from the eastern part of the perimeter. More bad news also came that day, December 5. He was informed by the Commando Supremo in Rome—the Italian high command—that he could expect no reinforcements for a month, and during this time only the barest essential supplies would be shipped across the Mediterranean.

Now Rommel had only one option: to withdraw from Tobruk entirely. This withdrawal began on the night of December 7. With the DAK covering the open desert flank, he pulled back to Gazala. The British followed along, and it soon became clear that the DAK's remaining there would be foolhardy; the German line was only twelve miles long and could be easily outflanked. Rommel therefore resolved to pull out of Cyrenaica altogether. The Italian high command objected vehemently, pointing out that he had a duty to protect the Italians living there. Rommel retorted that his mind was made up; he would, if need be, take merely the German element of Panzer Group Africa with him and leave the Italian formations to their fate. At this the Italians backed down. While the infantry divisions moved rearward along the coast road via Benghazi, the mobile formations cut across the base of the Cyrenaica bulge. Far to the east the frontier garrisons of Bardia and Halfaya continued to hold out, but they were forced to surrender on January 2 and 17 respectively.

Rommel came to rest at Agedabia on Christmas Day. The British had done little to interfere with his withdrawal since they, too, had become bedeviled by supply problems. They did mount an attack on Agedabia on December 27, but Rommel held them, and they withdrew after three days. Nevertheless, Agedabia could also be outflanked, and so Rommel withdrew farther west to Mersa Brega and by January 12 was firm on this position, where he had been almost a year earlier. Thus 1941 had been a year of mixed fortunes for Rommel. It had started spectacularly, but he had been eventually foiled through his failure to capture Tobruk. His determination to reach the Suez Canal was by no means diminished; heartened by better news on the supply front, he was already preparing for his next move.

CHAPTER 4

Rommel's High Tide

ON JANUARY 5, 1942, ROMMEL RECEIVED FIFTY-FOUR new tanks and twenty armored cars, which were landed at Tripoli. An additional bonus was that his intelligence on the state of the British forces in Cyrenaica had received a boost from an unlikely source, the U.S. military attaché in Cairo. After Hitler declared war on the United States the previous month, the Americans and British had agreed that defeating Germany had priority over defeating Japan. Hence there was great U.S. interest on what was happening in North Africa. Colonel Bonner Fellers established very good relations with the British high command and sent lengthy reports back to Washington, D.C., on the situation as the British saw it and their future intentions. Both the Germans and the Italians had managed to crack the code he was using, and his messages were passed to Rommel. They were to be invaluable to him during the next six months.

Through Fellers and radio intercepts Rommel learned that the British intention was to launch an offensive into Tripolitania. This was going to take time to prepare, however. Their supply lines were again stretched, and as had been the case a year earlier, the formations that had taken part in the recent offensive had had to withdraw to refit. In terms of armor, the newly arrived 1st Armored Division was still finding its feet and only had one armored brigade in place. The other division in Cyrenaica, the 4th Indian, had its brigades dispersed. Rommel had numerical superiority, but it clearly would not last. Now that he had received replacement tanks he therefore decided to attack immediately. Surprise was crucial, and he informed neither the German nor Italian high commands of his intentions, especially since the latter was not good at keeping secrets. In essence, Benghazi was his immediate objective, and he intended that the 90th Light Division, supported by tanks from the 21st Panzer Division, would advance up the coast road and secure the port. Simultaneously, the DAK would strike northeastward to Msus.

On the eve of the attack Rommel received some good news from Berlin. He had been awarded the Swords to the Oak Leaves of his Knight's Cross. Then, on January 21, he noted in his diary: "After carefully weighing the pros and cons, I've decided to take the risk. I have complete faith that God is keeping a protective hand over us and that He will give us victory."[1] The attack began at 5:00 P.M. the same evening.

The British were taken entirely by surprise, not only by the timing, but by the way the Germans operated their tanks and antitank guns. The latter would leapfrog forward while the tanks provided cover from static hull-down positions. The antitank guns would then take up position and, in turn, provide support for the tanks as they moved forward. The pace at which this maneuver was carried out proved too much for the British armor, which continually had to give ground, as well as suffering casualties. As Rommel remarked in a hurried line to Lucie, "Our opponents are getting out as though they'd been stung."[2] Agedabia fell to the 90th Light Division on the morning of the twenty-second. Rommel then adjusted his original plan. The 90th Light was to head east of Benghazi so as to trap its garrison as it sought to escape to the north or east while the DAK established a blocking line running from Agedabia northeast to Antelat and then to Saunnu. Two days later, with disorganization growing among the British, Rommel had another change of heart. While he appreciated that his low fuel stocks limited his scope, he believed that if he moved quickly he could literally stampede the British out of Cyrenaica. But on January 23 General Ugo Cavallero arrived at Rommel's headquarters from the Italian High Command in Rome. He expressed his displeasure at Rommel's unilateral action, but Rommel refused to be dissuaded, assuring the Italians that he was using largely German troops. On January 25 he personally led a dash on Msus, overtaking numerous vehicles of the 1st Armored Division. He then feinted toward Mechili, adding to the British confusion. With fuel now very short and the British withdrawing eastward as fast as they could go, Rommel turned on Benghazi, which fell into his hands on January 29. The British withdrew back to the Gazala–Bir Hacheim line, where Rommel had temporarily halted after withdrawing from Tobruk the previous December, and began to construct fortified defenses. Rommel followed up and halted in front of this line on February 4. As he commented, the campaign had gone "like greased lightning."[3]

There was now a four months' pause. Both sides intended to mount future attacks, but for the present neither was able to. The Italians were still not impressed with what Rommel had done. Fearing that the British might thrust along the base of the Cyrenaican Bulge and cut Rommel off, they wanted him to withdraw, but he ignored them. In retaliation they withdrew one of their corps from his command. He was, however, cheered by the fact that his command was now designated Panzer Army Africa and that he was promoted to colonel general. On February 15 Rommel flew to Rome at the start of what would be four weeks' leave. The war diary of the 90th Light Division commented: "Everybody breathes a huge sigh of relief, and looks forward to the coming days of calm."[4] Before going home, he visited Hitler at his headquarters at Rastenburg in East Prussia, the so-called Wolf's Lair, and was decorated with his Swords. When Rommel did get home he was, by his own admission, very restless and constantly wondering about the situation in Libya. Consequently, it was hardly a relaxing leave, either for him, Lucie, or his thirteen-year-old son Manfred, to whom he was very attached.

Rommel returned to North Africa on March 19. While at the Wolf's Lair he had been able to discuss his thoughts on the future of the North African campaign. He envisaged advancing into Egypt and, from there, moving up through Palestine and Syria and eventually threatening the Russians in the Caucasus. Hitler was sympathetic, since he also had his eyes on the Caucasus, especially its oil fields, and an assault south into this region was in his mind for the main effort on the Eastern Front for the summer. Conscious of the threat that Malta was posing to his supply lines across the Mediterranean, Rommel also asked if the island could be subjected to heavy bombardment from the air, to which Hitler assented.

Rommel was thus in good spirits on his return, and even more so that his stocks of matériel were beginning to build up. The only discouraging factor was that OKH had warned him that, in view of the demands of the Eastern Front, he could expect little in the way of reinforcements. Nevertheless, on March 29 he briefed his staff and senior commanders, stating that he intended to attack again in May and that the object was to seize Tobruk. This plan accorded with what his superiors had in mind. In mid-April, while at his Alpine retreat of Berchtesgaden, Hitler saw Mussolini, Cavallero, and Field Marshal Albert Kesselring, a Luftwaffe officer whom Hitler had appointed commander-in-chief South, responsible for the Mediterranean theater. They agreed that Rommel could attack in May, but that he was to advance no farther than Tobruk.

The detailed planning for the assault on the Gazala Line could now begin. Its defenses were based on a series of brigade-sized "boxes," positions each occupied by an infantry brigade and surrounded by minefields and barbed wire. They appeared formidable, although there was a weakness in that some boxes were too far apart from one another to provide mutual support by fire. Behind the boxes themselves was the British armor, ready to deal with any penetrations. The line itself ran for some fifty miles south to Bir Hacheim, but the armor was also ready to deal with any attempt to outflank it, although it was dispersed rather than concentrated. As Rommel was aware, the British, too, were preparing for an attack. His troops on one occasion told him they would attack on Easter Monday, April 6. In typical Rommel fashion he went to see for himself. With just one tank as an escort he drove toward the British defenses, but could see no obvious indicators that an attack was imminent. He was then shelled. A splinter penetrated the windscreen of his vehicle and struck him in the chest, causing a large bruise. Discretion did overrule valor on this occasion and he withdrew. It did not deter him from carrying out further personal reconnaissance.

He had, however, formulated a plan. What he needed to do was to divert the attention of the British armor to enable his own to get behind the Gazala Line and make for Tobruk. He thus decided that a frontal attack would be made by his infantry, while the mobile forces swept round the south, trapped the Eighth Army, destroyed it, and then moved on to Tobruk. The greatest risk was that the supply line of the mobile forces would be very vulnerable, and there was a very real danger that the Axis armor would run out of fuel and find itself stranded behind British lines. Rommel, however, was convinced that the British would not be able to match the tempo of his operations, especially at the tactical level; in the field of interarms cooperation the British were still well behind the Germans.

During the preparation period Rommel was, as usual, tireless. He visited every unit, including those concerned with logistics. His optimism percolated throughout his command. "The German and Italian soldiers just light up when Rommel comes," noted his interpreter Lieutenant Wilfried Armbruster.[5] He also enjoyed the publicity he was continuing to receive in Germany. He was often referred to on the radio as "our popular hero, Colonel General Rommel,"[6] and was beginning to receive a considerable amount of fan mail. At the same time, he had also gained the respect of the British troops, to the extent that Auchinleck had felt forced in March 1942 to issue a statement to his subordinate commanders which read: "There is a real danger that our friend Rommel will turn into a bogeyman. . . . He is not superhuman—energetic and capable as he is."[7]

On May 12 Rommel gave the details of his plan to his senior commanders. The attack in the Gazala area was to be

commanded by Crüwell and would be made by the four infantry divisions of the Italian X and XXI Corps, together with
two regimental groups from the 90th Light Division and designated the 15th Rifle Brigade. It would begin at 2:00 P.M.,
and was expected to penetrate to a depth of some ten miles. A
panzer battalion and another of captured British tanks would
then simulate a major armored thrust to draw the British
armor toward Gazala. Rommel himself would lead the mobile
force (the 15th and 21st Panzer Divisions, 90th Light Division
less the 15th Rifle Brigade, and the Ariete armored and Trieste
motorized divisions). It would begin its move round the
Gazala line at dawn the next day. He expected to destroy the
Eighth Army in two days and then move on to Tobruk. He decided to move on May 26 and wrote to Lucie that morning:
"We're launching a decisive attack today. It will be hard, but I
have full confidence that my army will win it. After all, they
know what battle means. There is no need to tell you how I
will go into it. I intend to demand of myself the same as I expect from each of my officers and men."[8]

The British expected a German attack. Both Ultra, the
cover name for coded German signals decrypted at Bletchley
Park in England, and radio intercepts pointed to it, but Ultra
tended to indicate an attack possibly in the center of the line,
while intercepts and information gained from prisoners
pointed to a possible move by the DAK round Bir Hacheim.
Consequently Auchinleck and the Eighth Army commander
Neil Ritchie kept open minds. The only significant difference
between the two was over the deployment of the two armored
divisions. Auchinleck wanted both to be in the north so that
they were best placed to cover Tobruk whichever option Rommel might adopt, while Ritchie actually had the 1st Armored
Division just south of Tobruk and the 7th Armored Division
ten miles farther to the south. Ritchie was convinced that they

were in the right position to deal with every eventuality, and Auchlinleck reluctantly accepted this even though the armor was now dispersed rather than concentrated.

The DAK attack began as planned on the afternoon of May 26. It did not go according to plan. The attack in the north soon became bogged down by the minefields and so did not draw the British armor toward it as Rommel had hoped. During this time Rommel and his mobile troops moved south, but were spotted by British armored cars, which reported the movement and so Ritchie placed his armor on alert. At 4:30 A.M. on the twenty-seventh they passed round the Gazala Line, knocking two British motor brigades out of the way. They were then confronted by two armored brigades, but managed to drive them back and in the process overran the headquarters of the 7th Armored Division. All did not go Rommel's way, however. The British had a new antitank gun, the six-pounder, and a new tank, the American-built M3 General Grant. Both proved more effective antitank weapons than the British had hitherto possessed, and one-third of Rommel's tanks had been destroyed or incapacitated. The 90th Light Division had also become separated from the panzer divisions, and British forces were exploiting the resultant gap and attacking supply columns. What gave Rommel hope, however, was that the British tank attacks had been launched piecemeal and he had been able to defeat them one by one. He therefore planned to bring the 90th Light, which was in the El Adem area, back to join the DAK and continue to push northward next day.

It started badly. Shortly after dawn Rommel's own command post was attacked by British tanks, but he and his vehicles managed to get out of range. He went off to visit the Italian XX Motorized Corps and ordered it to follow behind the DAK. Then came news that the 90th Light Division was experiencing difficulties. Harried by British tanks and attacked from the air, it was forced to take up a defensive position six miles east of Bir el Harmat and was thus unable to join the DAK, which had also gone over to the defensive. Then came news that part of the 15th Panzer Division had run out of ammunition. Rommel went up to see what was happening and reached a hill ten miles north of Bir el Harmat, from which he could view the battle as the DAK continued to repulse British attacks. He commented that the black smoke clouds from burning vehicles gave the landscape "a curious sinister beauty."[9] He decided to follow the route he had used to lead supply columns to the DAK early the following morning. On his way back to his headquarters he had clashes with both a British and an Italian column. He also found that his headquarters had been attacked, as well as some of the DAK's supply columns. During the night the 90th Light Division had managed to move closer to Bir el Harmat, and Rommel deployed the Ariete to fill the gap still existing between it and the DAK. At dawn on May 29 Rommel set out for the DAK once more, this time bringing up its supply columns. They arrived just in time, since the tanks were by now all but immobilized through lack of fuel and were again under attack. Rommel remained with them for the rest of the day. Darkness brought an end to the fighting, with the armor of both sides withdrawing into laager, or tank parks, as was the normal practice.

Reviewing the situation that night, Rommel could gain satisfaction from the fact that he had established a reasonably secure position east of the southern part of the Gazala Line and astride the Trigh el Abd, a track that ran southeast to El Gubi. Maintaining delivery of supplies to his forces there was more problematical. Bir Hacheim, which he had expected to fall quickly, had not done so and was being obstinately held by a Free French brigade. He had tried to send the Trieste

Division through the Gazala Line north of Bir Hacheim so as to shorten his supply line, but it had become entrapped in minefields. As for the attack in the north, it had kept the defenders pinned down, but had still been unable to break into the defenses. Crüwell himself had been shot down in his Fieseler Storch and was now a British prisoner. Kesselring, who had arrived on a visit, had, however, stepped into the breach and taken over command of this part of the front. Rommel's conclusion was that it was too risky to continue to attack east of the Gazala Line until he had improved the supply situation. He therefore gave orders for the DAK, Ariete, and 90th Light Division to remain on the defensive, but on a shortened line facing northeast. Elements of the 90th Light and the panzer divisions would, in the meantime, break into the Gazala Line from the east, while the Italian X Corps did so from the west. The idea was to establish a corridor through which supplies could flow and isolate the Free French at Bir Hacheim.

The new break-in operation began next day, May 30. The Italian X Corps and the force attacking from the east managed to quickly clear a lane through the minefields, and Rommel was able to use it to meet Kesselring and the commander of X Corps and explain to them that he now intended to clean up the southern part of the Gazala Line prior to continuing the attack northward. Apart from the Free French at Bir Hacheim, the principal obstacle to this operation was the box held by the British 150th Brigade (part of the 50th [Northumbrian] Division) and supported by a brigade of infantry tanks. Rommel began to attack it on May 31. It took forty-eight hours of grueling fighting to capture the box. Rommel described it as "the toughest resistance imaginable" and said that the "defense was conducted with considerable skill and, as usual, the British fought to the last round."[10] He lost two invaluable members of his staff here. Gause, his chief of staff, was hit by a shell splinter, and Colonel Siegfried Westphal, his operations officer, was badly wounded by mortar fire while standing with Rommel. Fritz Bayerlein, the DAK's chief of staff, took Gause's place. There was, however, no pause. On the night of June 1–2 Rommel turned against Bir Hacheim. It was to prove an even tougher battle than that against the 150th Brigade. The Free French held out for no less than ten days, and Rommel himself personally led a number of assaults. Eventually, with their ammunition virtually exhausted, the defenders exfiltrated their way out and linked up with the 7th Motor Brigade, which had been harassing Rommel's supply lines.

During the first few days of these operations the bulk of the Eighth Army did little, apart from one or two piecemeal attacks that were easily repelled by the DAK and Ariete. This enabled Rommel to rebuild his tank strength, which had fallen to 130 from its total of 320 at the outset of the offensive. Ritchie, however, was preparing an attack into the Cauldron, as the area of the Gazala Line now held by Rommel came to be called. It came on June 5. An infantry tank brigade attacked from the north, while one armored and two infantry brigades did so from the east. It initially made good progress, with the Ariete in the center being driven back. Artillery fire brought the northern British prong to a halt and the eastern attack was foiled when the two panzer divisions, together with a reserve battle group led by Rommel himself, fell on its flanks. The British suffered heavy losses and Rommel could then turn his attention once more to Bir Hacheim. When it fell on June 11 the time had finally arrived for him to resume his advance northward.

The northern part of the Gazala Line was still standing firm and held by the 1st South African Division and the remaining two brigades of the 50th Division. They were supported by the

32nd Army Tank Brigade (infantry tanks). Facing Rommel's armor were three brigade boxes situated along the line of the east-west Trigh Capuzzo. In the west the 201st Guards Brigade held a position called Knightsbridge. Some fifteen miles to the east was the 29th Indian Infantry Brigade just southwest of El Adem, and beyond it was the 21st Indian Infantry Brigade. Between the Guards and the Indians were three armored brigades (the 2nd, 4th, and 22nd). Rommel himself set off on the afternoon of June 11 with the 15th Panzer and 90th Light Divisions, together with a reconnaissance battalion. By the evening they were some six miles south of El Adem. The following morning they fought a running battle with the 2nd Armored Brigade and inflicted heavy casualties on it. By noon El Adem was in German hands, but the 29th Indian Brigade still held out in its box. Simultaneously, a battle group from the 21st Panzer Division began to drive east, as a result of which the British armor, now joined by the 32nd Army Tank Brigade, was beginning to be squeezed between it and the 15th Panzer. Rommel, wanting as usual to see for himself, went up to El Adem to watch the 90th Light attacking the Indians. He then tried to get through to the 15th Panzer, but his tactical headquarters came under heavy fire and was pinned down for a considerable period. The day culminated for Rommel in being bombed by Stukas, which had been forced to ditch their bombs on being attacked by RAF fighters. Tank battles continued the following day, June 13, as the Axis forces pressed the British north of Trigh Capuzzo. The counterattacks became weaker as British tank casualties rose and the Guards were forced to evacuate the Knightsbridge box. By the end of the day Ritchie accepted that he must withdraw from what remained of the Gazala Line. He now aimed to hold a line running south from Tobruk.

During June 14–15 the Eighth Army withdrew. Rommel tried to cut off the formations withdrawing from the Gazala

Line, but his troops, now exhausted, were unable to do so. Both Auchinleck and Churchill wanted Ritchie to hold on to Tobruk and not to withdraw east of it, but he considered his forces too disorganized for this to be possible and began to withdraw to the frontier. Tobruk itself was held by the 2nd South African Division, but it only had two brigades, what remained of the 201st Guards Brigade, and the 32nd Army Tank Brigade. The defenses had been allowed to deteriorate, and many of the mines had been removed to strengthen the Gazala Line. Rommel isolated the fortress on June 18 and two days later attacked it. While the Italian XXI Corps and the 15th Rifle Brigade made a feint from the southwest, the main assault by the DAK and XX Corps came in from the southeast. The latter was preceded by a massive air attack. This time Tobruk fell in virtually a day. Some strongpoints offered resistance, but otherwise the defenders were numbed. That evening an officer saw Rommel and Bayerlein eating a hasty meal of captured British rations by the light of a flickering candle. "Only his eyes gleam with deep and unalterable happiness."[11] Rommel drove into Tobruk shortly after dawn the next day and took the surrender of General Hendrik Klopper, the South African commander. He then issued an order of the day praising the efforts of his men over the past month. It ended: "Now for the complete destruction of the enemy. We will not rest until we have shattered the last remnants of the British Eighth Army. During the days to come, I shall call on you for one more great effort to bring this about."[12] It was to prove easier said than done.

The news of the fall of Tobruk was announced on German radio at midday the same day, June 21. Newsreels featuring Rommel were immediately rushed out to cinemas throughout the country. He was once again the hero of the hour. His promotion to field marshal was announced; he was the youngest officer to hold the rank at the time. Yet Rommel was in no mood to stop and savor the glory and the vast amounts of supplies that had fallen into his hands. He was already organizing his next advance eastward.

Rommel had been told, of course, that having captured Tobruk, he was to halt. The next stage in the Axis Mediterranean strategy was to be the capture of Malta. In spite of the pounding from the air that the island had suffered during the past few months and a serious shortage of supplies, it continued to hold out. The Axis air forces had been unable to achieve air supremacy, which was a vital prerequisite for an air and seaborne assault. To Rommel the situation was clear. He had the Eighth Army on the ropes, and it would be madness to allow it any breathing space in which to recover. The path to the Suez Canal lay open, and he meant to take it, especially since his supply situation had been much boosted by what he had captured in Tobruk. He managed to get Kesselring to see matters the same way and also sent a personal letter to Hitler. This was timely, since he received a letter from Marshal Cavallero in Rome at the same time. Cavallero once more emphasized the need to capture Malta. He stated that the Italian navy was very short of oil and hence could only escort a limited number of convoys to North Africa and those that were sent were still unloading their supplies at Tripoli, Benghazi being considered too risky, since it was within easy air range of Malta. Hitler, though, took Rommel's side and told Mussolini that the invasion of Egypt was to go ahead.

Rommel had already issued his orders; his troops, having inched up to the frontier, crossed it on June 23. On the British side Ritchie made no attempt to hold the frontier and withdrew to Mersa Matruh, 150 miles to the east. There defenses were hastily constructed. Auchinleck did not like this plan because the Mersa Matruh line could be outflanked in exactly the same way as the Gazala Line. He was looking at a much more defensible position, a hundred miles farther east, at El Alamein. True, it was close to the Nile Delta, but it had the great advantage of being anchored in the south by the virtually impassable Qattara Depression. This meant that Rommel could only get through it frontally, and hence the British had a much better chance of stopping him there. If this failed, Auchinleck would withdraw to the Suez Canal and, if need be, continue the fight in Palestine. What was essential was to keep the army intact; to commit it to an all-out effort at Mersa Matruh would as likely as not destroy it. Consequently, on June 25 he sacked Ritchie and took charge of the Eighth Army himself. It was, however, too late to alter Ritchie's plans, and so he intended merely to buy time at Mersa Matruh before withdrawing everything to El Alamein.

Determined not to allow the British any respite, Rommel approached Mersa Matruh on the following day. Auchinleck had already ordered his XXX Corps back to the El Alamein Line and Mersa Matruh itself was held by X Corps, with XIII Corps to its south. The latter consisted of the New Zealand Division and the 1st Armored Division, but coordination at all levels from corps downward was lacking, and there were gaps in the defenses. Rommel duly attacked on June 26, having captured additional stocks of fuel en route from the frontier. His plan was to elbow the 1st Armored Division out of the way and then encircle Matruh itself. While the DAK dealt with the British armor, the 90th Light Division drove through south of the New Zealanders and then turned north and established itself astride the coast road. Two Italian infantry divisions in trucks followed in the wake of the 90th Light to close the ring, with others establishing a perimeter on the west and southwest sides of Mersa Matruh. The Brescia and Pavia Divisions in the south moved too slowly and the

New Zealand Division began to break out during the night. Parts of X Corps also attempted the same and the 90th Light fought all night to try to prevent them escaping eastward. On 28 June Rommel began to break into Mersa Matruh, while the DAK continued to advance, securing Fuqa forty miles beyond by the end of the day. The situation was highly confused, though, with British and German columns racing in the same direction. Mersa Matruh fell the next day, yielding 6,000 prisoners and much booty. Rommel wrote to Lucie: "Now that the battle of Mersa Matruh has also been won and our leading troops are only 125 miles from Alexandria. There'll be a few more battles to fight before we reach our goal, but I think the worst is well behind us."[13] It was overly optimistic, especially since a good proportion of the Mersa Matruh defenders had got away, and the Eighth Army, albeit "brave but baffled," was still an entity. Furthermore, the British Desert Air Force was very active.

Rommel approached the El Alamein Line on June 30. His troops were now virtually at the end of their tether. They were exhausted. Their numerical strength was also low. The two panzer divisions had only some 500 motorized infantry between them and possessed a mere 55 tanks still running, while the Italians had only 30. The other bedrock formation, the 90th Light, was down to 1,500 effective infantry. Artillery, especially Italian, was also now well below strength. The divisions had sufficient fuel, for a while at least, but transport, much of it now captured from the British, was in short supply, and was being constantly harried by the Desert Air Force. Rommel, however, was certain that his opponent was in an even groggier state.

Certainly the Eighth Army's degree of disorganization, after its pell-mell retreat, was much greater than that of Panzer Army Africa, but it was still a fighting force. Auchinleck saw El

Alamein itself, even though it was little more than a small railway station, as the fulcrum of his defense. It was held as a box by a South African brigade. The remaining two brigades of the 1st South African Division were deployed south of this box as mobile columns and supported by two armored brigades. Rommel was expected to try to cut off El Alamein, and the idea was that the mobile formations would prevent him from doing this. To the south lay the dominant Ruweisat Ridge and to ensure that he passed north of this an Indian brigade was deployed at its western end. South again of the Ruweisat Ridge lay XIII Corps. The New Zealand Division had one brigade forward and the remainder back on the Deir el Munassib feature. In the more broken terrain of the far south lay the 5th Indian Division and the remains of the 7th Armored Division. The British had some 250 tanks of all types available and had a major advantage in that their lines of communication were the shortest they had ever been in North Africa.

Rommel gave out his orders for the attack on the afternoon of June 30. His plan was much the same as the one he had used at Mersa Matruh. His intelligence was, however, very inaccurate. He believed that there was an entire division in the El Alamein box and that there was a complete Indian division in front of the Ruweisat Ridge. He also thought that there was an armored division in front of the New Zealanders. In his haste he had had little time to reconnoiter the British position. The 90th Light Division was to cut the coast road east of El Alamein while the DAK swung southward in front of the Ruweisat Ridge to keep XIII Corps away from the main battle. The Italian XX Corps was to tie down the armor supposedly in front of the New Zealanders, and their two infantry corps were to hold open the shoulders of the breach made by the 90th Light. Zero hour was to be 3:00 A.M. No sooner had Rommel finished giving his orders than there was a bombing raid, which wounded Rommel's soldier servant. It was not an encouraging portent.

Matters went wrong from the start. Although the 90th Light Division attacked on time, it veered too far northward and ran up against the El Alamein box. When daylight came, it was pinned down by accurate artillery fire and also had to endure a sandstorm. It was too much for some of the exhausted riflemen, and they turned and fled, something that had never happened before to German troops in Africa. They were got back into the line. The division then moved farther south and dug in with a view to continuing its attack in the afternoon. The DAK also experienced problems. Poor trafficability, delays in resupply, the sandstorm, and an air attack meant that it was not until 8:00 A.M. that the attack got going. It then ran into the Indians on the Ruweisat Ridge. They Indians fought hard and not until evening were they eventually overrun. Rommel himself was with the DAK for the first part of the day. Hearing that that the 90th Light was in difficulties, he took a reserve battle group to help it in its next attempt to get through to the coast. As soon as they began to move forward, there was another barrage of British artillery fire. The attack came to a halt almost as soon as it started, with Rommel and Bayerlein having to lie out in the open for two hours. Once the fire slackened, he returned to his headquarters, ordering the 90th Light to make another attempt that night.

During the night Rommel had news that the British Mediterranean Fleet had left its base at Alexandria. It dispersed to Port Said, Beirut, and Haifa. On that same day, 29 June, elements of HQ Middle East in Cairo withdrew to Palestine and there was a wholesale burning of confidential documents. The withdrawal of the British fleet reinforced Rommel's determination to continue the attack: "I was convinced that a breakthrough over a wide front by my force would result in complete panic."[14] Yet the 90th Light again made little progress during the night, and so Rommel ordered the DAK to take over its original mission of cutting the coast road. Meanwhile, Auchinleck had been made aware of Rommel's plan, courtesy of Ultra, and decided to wrest the initiative from him by getting his armor to attack westward. The DAK did not begin to move north until the afternoon, and then immediately ran into two British armored brigades. The fighting went on until dusk, with both sides suffering casualties. The British were unable to drive the DAK back but had stopped its advance. More seriously, the Germans had a mere twenty-eight fit tanks by the end of the day. The attack continued next day, with the DAK advancing along the Ruweisat Ridge and the Ariete giving support in the south. The DAK did make some progress, but not enough, and suffered further tank losses, largely thanks to the 1st Armored Division. Worse, the Ariete was attacked in the flank by the New Zealanders and all but broke. That evening Rommel finally realized that his troops had reached the end of their tether. He, too, was exhausted.

Early on July 4 he gave orders for the DAK to withdraw, its place being taken by Italian infantry formations. Auchinleck, sensing that the Axis forces were going over to the defensive, ordered XIII Corps to attack northwest in an effort to cut them off. Fatigue on the British side was by now almost as endemic as it was with their opponents. The orders got watered down, and there was little urgency. The only incident of note was that the 1st Armored Division did catch the 15th Panzer Division during the initial stages of its withdrawal and caused some alarm, but a hastily deployed antitank gun screen brought the British tanks to a halt.

The next few days saw both sides reinforcing. Welcome for Rommel was the arrival of 2,000 German infantrymen, who were flown in to Tobruk from Crete; they provided the nucleus of what would become the 164th Light Division. Some Italian reinforcements also arrived, having been sent up from Tripoli, and he was also promised an additional three Italian divisions. There were no more tanks forthcoming, but a few were repaired and redelivered to the front. On the British side, the 9th Australian Division arrived from Syria, and the tank strength was built up to 200. Auchinleck gave up his attempts to strike a decisive blow with XIII Corps from the southeast. Instead, he would attack southwest out of the El Alamein box.

With his troops finally enjoying a short respite, Rommel also planned another attack. He identified the weak point in the British line as the area held by the New Zealanders south of the Ruweisat Ridge. Auchinleck got wind of this through Ultra and withdrew the forward New Zealand brigade from its rather exposed box. Rommel duly attacked on July 9 and thought that he had found a gap. He sent the 90th Light Division and a reconnaissance battalion to advance eastward to establish a route that could take the Axis forces to Eighth Army's rear. In the early hours on July 10, as this operation was proceeding, there was an ominous rumble of gunfire to the north. It marked the beginning of the British attack from El Alamein.

The artillery barrage that preceded the attack was of an intensity seldom seen in the Desert War. It took the two Italian divisions holding the coast totally by surprise and a considerable number were made prisoner. Even more serious for Rommel was that his radio intercept unit was overrun, with its commander and many of the operators killed and their codebooks captured. Thus his main source of intelligence had been lost. Rommel himself was forward with the DAK and in the abandoned New Zealand box. In his absence

Friedrich von Mellenthin, his operations officer at Panzer Army headquarters, immediately sent forward the newly arrived infantry from Crete to restore the situation, together with some machine gunners and antiaircraft guns. Rommel, too, as soon as he heard what was happening, halted the operation south of Ruweisat and led a battle group from the 15th Panzer Division toward the sounds of battle. These two moves enabled the British attack to be brought to a halt, but Rommel was now aware that the combat power of the Italians was declining rapidly. Accordingly, he decided on another attack on the El Alamein box. This time the 21st Panzer Division was to cut it off and break into it. Rommel decided to mount the attack at midday on July 13, choosing this time because the heat shimmer would make it difficult for the British to clearly identify targets. Stukas supported the attack and a providential sandstorm blew up. The initial progress seemed promising, and Rommel began to harbor hopes that the coast road would be cut, but by late afternoon the situation had changed for the worse. The infantry had initially formed up too far behind the tanks, and cooperation between the two and the combat engineers was lacking. Effective British artillery fire also played its part, and the attack ground to a halt. A bitterly disappointed Rommel ordered the attackers back to their start line. He renewed the battle next day, this time attacking the Australians, who were holding the lodgment as a result of the attack out of the box. Pounded by artillery and from the air, the Germans again made limited progress.

Rommel intended to resume the assault the next day, but that night the New Zealanders mounted an attack against the western part of the Ruweisat Ridge and threw the Italian X Corps into disarray. The New Zealanders were supposed to be supported by the 1st Armored Division, but it was late in

moving off. Rommel again summoned the DAK, and it counterattacked the New Zealand brigade on the western end of
the ridge. The British armor stood back, waiting for the right
moment to counterattack and believing that the New Zealanders could look after themselves. Unfortunately for them, their
antitank guns were short of ammunition and they were overrun. The British armor finally came into action and prevented
the DAK from moving any farther eastward. Each side made
local attacks during the next two days, but Rommel was by
now ever more conscious that the British were growing in
strength whereas he was literally scraping the barrel to hold his
line. A visit from Kesselring and Cavallero on July 17 did not
improve his spirits. To them he stated how desperate his
supply situation was becoming, but Cavallero appeared to
think that he was exaggerating, although he did eventually
agree to make some improvements and again promised more
Italian formations.

Auchinleck now prepared to mount another attack. Rommel, accepting that Panzer Army Africa was no longer capable
of meaningful offensive operations, was concentrating on improving his defenses, especially by laying minefields. On July
21 he sent a long signal to OKH that was picked up by Ultra.
He stated that he believed that he could prevent a major
British breakthrough, but until the rest of the 164th Light
Division arrived and he had done more work in his defenses,
he would remain anxious. He was particularly concerned that
he no longer had the resources to form a proper mobile reserve and also spoke of his severe shortage of antitank and artillery guns. He reiterated his severe supply situation, which
was being aggravated by constant British bombing of Tobruk
and Mersa Matruh. He was also angry that too much shipping space was being taken up by Italian rather than German
reinforcements. All this was very encouraging for Auchinleck,

who now intended to use XIII Corps to break through the Axis defenses and pursue Rommel to Fuqa while making feint attacks in the extreme south. XXX Corps in the north would also make local attacks to keep the enemy tied down. The attack began on July 22, but a breakthrough was beyond the Eighth Army's capabilities at this stage, with the Australian, Indian, and New Zealand troops spearheading the attack, again not receiving the planned armored support. But the British pressure was such that at 5:00 P.M. Rommel sent a desperate signal to Commando Supremo in Rome. It warned that "our losses have been very heavy, particularly in the rifle units, and the position is very critical. It is questionable whether the whole front will be able to hold out any longer against such heavy pressure."[15] Subsequent days saw the British attempting to further wear down their opponents, but they were running out of reserves and were also too tired to carry on. Therefore, on July 27 Auchinleck finally called a halt. The first battle of El Alamein, a prolonged slogging match between two increasingly groggy opponents, was over. The British had stopped Rommel's advance to the Suez Canal, but they had failed to drive him back, and a temporary stalemate ensued.

Rommel remained anxious for the next couple of days, even going so far as to issue a special order on the evening of July 29: "I order every man—including those at HQ—to remain at his post and not to retreat. Retreat means destruction. . . . Anyone deserting his post is to be charged with cowardice in the face of the enemy."[16] A few days later he was breathing a little easier, but in a letter to Lucie on August 2 he noted the amount of sickness, especially among older officers. "Even I am feeling very tired and limp, though I have got a chance to look after myself a bit just at the moment."[17] There was, however, no question of Rommel's taking leave, for he was

in a race against time. He knew that the British would be reinforcing and was determined to make another attempt to reach
the Suez Canal before they became too strong. He and his staff
estimated that the Eighth Army was likely to receive substan-
tial additions. Because of the Axis air threat the Mediterranean
was too dangerous; these had to come via the Cape of Good
Hope on the tip of South Africa. Rommel therefore calculated
that they would not arrive until the beginning of September.
He therefore needed to strike before then and selected a target
date of August 26. This gave him a bare four weeks to build up
his own strength, including supplies, so as to have a reasonable
chance of making a successful attack. There was still the problem that the Italians were taking up an unfair proportion of
shipping space. Rommel blamed much of this on General
Enno von Rintelen, the German military attaché in Rome,
who was supposed to negotiate shipping space with the Italians. He was especially incensed that an Italian infantry division, the Pistoia, had arrived in country two weeks early, while
he was still awaiting two-thirds of the 164th Division and the
Ramcke Parachute Brigade, which had also been promised to
him. There was, too, a serious shortage of noncommissioned
officers, especially tank commanders. Nevertheless, by the
middle of the month matters had improved. Rommel felt that
he had a sufficiency of men and weapons to carry out his attack, and he expected to have enough fuel for ten days' operations. In an Assessment of the Situation dated August 15,
which he sent to OKW, OKH, Commando Supremo, and
Kesselring, he explained his intention. His plan was to pin
down the British in the northern part of the El Alamein defenses with attacks by the Italians while the German mobile
forces penetrated in the south, swept up to the coast, and then
encircled and destroyed the British forces in the area El

Alamein to Ruweisat. Thereafter he would continue the advance eastward.[18]

While Rommel was making his preparations for the renewal of the offensive there had been some radical changes on the British side. On August 3 Winston Churchill and the Chief of the Imperial General Staff, Sir Alan Brooke, had arrived in Cairo to examine the situation. Churchill had been disappointed that Auchinleck had closed down his attacks and did not intend to make another attempt to drive Rommel back until mid-September at the earliest. The upshot was a wholesale reorganization of the command structure in the Middle East. Auchinleck was relieved as commander in chief, Middle East, by the urbane General Sir Harold Alexander, while command of the Eighth Army was given to the dynamic General Sir Bernard Montgomery. Monty, as he was known throughout the British army, made his presence felt immediately. His first action was to destroy all plans for a withdrawal from the El Alamein Line and to tell his troops that there would be no further retreats; they were to stand and fight where they were. He was aware that Rommel intended to attack again and made his plan accordingly. This time the armor was not going to be allowed to counterattack; it had suffered too much in the past, especially from Rommel's antitank guns. Instead, it would be positioned on the Alam Halfa Ridge and the Axis tanks would be lured toward it and destroyed.

In the meantime there had been a crisis in the Axis camp. Rommel was far from well. The strain of the past nineteen months had caught up with him, and he was suffering chronic stomach and intestinal problems, colds, circulation problems, and general exhaustion. He was also prone to frequent fainting spells. Gause became extremely worried and had him medically examined. He and the doctor then sent a report back to

Germany stating that he was not fit to command the forth-coming offensive. Rommel himself believed that only one man had the necessary grasp of armored warfare to take over for him, Heinz Guderian. This officer was, however, temporarily out of favor with the regime, and the immediate reply from OKW was that he was "totally unacceptable."[19] Rommel therefore decided that he had to remain in command, and another message was sent stating that his health had improved to the extent that he was capable of doing this, provided he had constant medical attention. It was also agreed that once the operation was completed, Rommel would be given an extended break at home. Lieutenant Alfred Berndt, who had originally been seconded from Joseph Goebbels' Propaganda Ministry and had been with Rommel throughout the campaign, wrote a reassuring letter to Lucie Rommel on August 26. He told her that he had arranged for Rommel to have his own cook, and that special food, considerably better than the normal ration that the field marshal usually ate, was being provided. Everything was being done to make certain that he looked after himself. "This sort of 'mothering' is not of course particularly easy with the Marshal and he has to know as little about it as possible. Being the man he is, he would deny himself any extra rations."[20]

That Rommel was not well was kept from his men, but his staff remained anxious. There was, too, another major problem—fuel. The promised additional stocks had been delayed, and the last of them would not now arrive until August 28. This meant that the attack had to be postponed to August 30. As it happened, the British intercepted and sank three tankers from this convoy. Even though Kesselring had provided some additional fuel from Luftwaffe stocks, it meant that Panzer Army Africa now had only enough for four rather than ten days' operations. Accordingly, on August 29 Rommel signaled OKW, OKH, and Commando Supremo to warn them that "it will not be possible to undertake more than a limited local operation, with the object of hitting the enemy forces in the Alamein position." Only if further fuel arrived would it be possible to exploit an initial success.[21] The attack would still take place the next day, and there were no fundamental changes to Rommel's original plan.

Rommel in France, summer 1940, and wearing the Knight's Cross and Pour Le Mérite. (Photo courtesy of the National Archives and Records Administration)

Rommel visiting the Italian Ariete Division during the 1941 siege of Tobruk. M13/40 tank in the background. (Photo courtesy of the Australian War Memorial; negative number 04932)

Rommel consults with Italian generals after his arrival in Libya in February 1941. (Photo courtesy of the National Archives and Records Administration)

Rommel in Tripoli, February 1941 (Photo courtesy of the Australian War Memorial; negative number PO 3998_002)

Rommel during one of his inspection tours of France, spring 1944. (Photo courtesy of the National Archives and Records Administration)

Rommel enjoys a rare drink. (Photo courtesy of the Australian War Memorial; negative number P0090_86)

CHAPTER 5

Star on the Wane

THE MORNING OF AUGUST 30, 1942, FOUND ROMMEL filled with anxiety. According to his doctor, Professor Forster, who met him when he emerged from the truck in which he slept, Rommel told him that his decision to attack again at El Alamein was "the hardest I have ever taken." He referred to events in Russia, where the German Army Group A was almost at its last gasp in the Caucasus and was attempting to advance on Grozny. If it failed in this and Rommel did not reach the Suez Canal, then, he indicated, it would be total defeat for Germany. He wrote, too, to Lucie of his worries over his shortages but put a brave face on his situation: "If our blow succeeds, it might go some way toward deciding the whole course of the war. If it fails, at least I hope to give the enemy a pretty thorough beating."[1] Rommel knew that he was taking a gamble. It was his last chance, and if he did not achieve an immediate breakthrough, he would be forced onto the defensive, since the British would have grown too strong for him to try again. He could not countenance the idea of withdrawal, and to merely remain where he was and do nothing but wait for the British to attack was against his nature. Yet he was also aware that his enemy had had time to recover; it was not the exhausted and disorganized army he had faced at the beginning of July. He also realized that he was facing a new Eighth Army commander, about whom he knew little. In these circumstances, given the disadvantages under which Rommel was laboring, including his uncertain health, only a very rash and desperate commander would have decided to attack.

Once darkness fell, the troops moved into position, and 10:00 P.M. was laid down as H-hour. Rommel's intention was that the DAK should advance thirty miles eastward during the night and then turn north into the Eighth Army's forward supply area. The Italian XX Corps would cover the DAK's flank, while the 90th Light Division was established a blocking position north of the Italians to prevent the British forces in the north from interfering. The DAK began its advance on time but immediately came across rough going, which slowed the columns and caused congestion. At 1:00 A.M. they hit a minefield, having covered little more than five miles. While they were grappling with the minefield, they came under air attack, wounding General Walther Nehring, the DAK commander. Mortar fire added to the din and killed George von Bismarck, commander of 21st Panzer Division. Eventually, shortly after 5:15 A.M., a bridgehead was established on the far side of the minefield. The DAK's progress was being monitored by the British 7th Motor Brigade (part of the 7th Armored Division), which was acting as a screening force. This brigade was now ordered to fall back behind a newly laid second minefield. This obstacle slowed the DAK's advance further. By 7:00 A.M. it had covered little more than ten miles, and any element of surprise had been totally lost. Rommel now came forward from his headquarters to see for himself how matters stood. To continue any farther east would merely expose his troops to heavy fire from the flank. He therefore gave orders for the 21st and 15th Panzer Divisions and XX Corps to turn northeast and assault the Alam Halfa Ridge and a hill feature to its east, both of which he now saw as the key terrain. The DAK needed to resupply, and so the attack did not resume until 1:00 P.M. Sandstorms, and the resultant softer sand, slowed progress. Alam Halfa itself was held by the newly arrived 44th (Home Counties) Division, with three armored brigades in support. The latter were ready to deploy to prepared fire positions, which they did in the late afternoon. This prevented Rommel's troops from reaching their objective and they went into laager at 6:30 P.M.

During the night the DAK and the Italian mobile divisions were subjected to heavy bombing. More worrying for Rommel, however, was the fuel situation. He had been promised further stocks by September 1, but another tanker had been sunk and none had arrived. Furthermore, his intelligence reported a significant increase in shipping in Alexandria Harbor, from which he deduced the arrival of significant reinforcements for the Eighth Army (it was deliveries of a new tank, the American M4 Sherman). With fuel now at a premium Rommel decided to continue the attack with just one division, the 15th Panzer. It managed to get close to its objective but was brought to a halt by British fire and virtually dry fuel tanks. The remainder of Rommel's mobile forces was subjected to continual bombing and shell fire throughout the day. The following night and September 2 brought the same punishment, with Rommel himself having yet another narrow escape when bomb splinters hit the slit trench in which he was sheltering. It must have been clear to Rommel by the evening of the first that the attack had failed and that he did not have the resources to pursue it further, yet his ability to make quick decisions appears to have deserted him, perhaps because he was still unwell. It was not until the evening of September 2 that he decided to pull his forces back to virtually their original start line, although he did retain the British-laid minefields in the south. This duly happened the next day, but Montgomery still refused to unleash his armor to exploit the Axis withdrawal since he was not prepared to risk heavy tank casualties.

The Battle of Alam Halfa restored the Eighth Army's morale and gave it faith in its new commander. For the Axis forces their dreams of reaching the fleshpots of Cairo and the Suez Canal had evaporated. Yet not a few on the Axis side believed that Rommel could have continued his attack. Kesselring was not pleased and was certain that the fuel problem could have been overcome by capturing British stocks. As he wrote after the war, "I am convinced that this battle would have been no problem for the 'old' Rommel."[2] But while his casualties in manpower had not been heavy—some 2,500 killed, wounded, and missing—and he had lost just 68 tanks, the 400 trucks that had been destroyed were more serious from the logistics point of view. As it was, he was now firmly on the defensive and issued orders for the defenses to be strengthened. He laid great faith in the construction of extensive minefields designed to bog down the eventual British attack. Then he would strike it from the flanks.

Uppermost in Rommel's mind was the need to get away and recuperate so that he could once again become fully fit. He had, however, to await the arrival of a temporary replacement. This was to be Georg Stumme, the very same officer whom Rommel had followed in command of the 7th Panzer Division in 1940 and who had gone on to command armored forces in Russia. Stumme was delighted to be back in the saddle after having been court-martialed for the loss of plans for Hitler's summer 1942 offensive in Russia. One of his staff officers had disobeyed a Hitler order not to carry secret documents when flying close to the front lines. His plane was shot down and the corps plans fell into Russian hands. Stumme was five years older than Rommel, but when he finally arrived on September 19, he was left in no doubt that he was merely a caretaker. Rommel gave him instructions over the improvement of the defenses and made it plain that if the British attacked, Rommel would fly back from Germany immediately.

Rommel departed Africa on September 23 and visited Mussolini in Rome to plead for increased supplies before flying on to Germany. He was not, however, able to go home immediately. Doubtless through an arrangement made by Lieutenant Berndt, his aide, Rommel went to stay with Joseph Goebbels and his family. His recent reverse in Egypt appeared to have had little effect on his value as a propaganda icon. Newsreel film shows him standing a little self-consciously with the six Goebbels children. He also kept Goebbels and his wife entertained with stories of his exploits in North Africa. On the last day of the month he went to the Reich Chancellery to be given his field marshal's baton by Hitler and then was guest of honor at a party rally held in the Berlin Sportpalast. There Hitler made a speech praising Rommel for his achievements. More important to Rommel, however, was the chance to plead for more resources. He was able to explain to Hitler the difficulties that he was laboring under and was very condemning of the Italians. Indeed, he was certain that it was Italian spies who had informed the British of his impending attack at Alam

Halfa and had caused the sinking of the vital oil tankers. Hitler was clearly sympathetic, and Rommel was able to inform Stumme that both the German leader and Mussolini agreed that the Axis forces should remain where they were in Egypt until they were strengthened. "The Führer has promised me that he's hoping to see that the panzer army gets every possible reinforcement, and above all the newest and biggest tanks, rocket projectors and antitank guns."[3] His confidence much boosted, Rommel attended a press conference three days later, at Goebbels' request, and told the assembled journalists: "Today we stand just fifty miles from Alexandria and Cairo, and we have the door to all Egypt in our hands. And we mean to do something with it, too! We haven't gone all that way just so as to get thrown back again. You can take that from me. What we have, we hang on to."[4] Then he boarded a plane for Vienna to be reunited at last with Lucie and his son, Manfred, and begin his cure.

In Egypt both sides continued their preparations. The Axis defenses, as planned by Rommel, were based on extensive minefields at the front and covered by small outposts. Some 2,000 yards to the rear lay the main defensive belt. This line was manned in such a way that every Italian unit had a German neighbor to stiffen it. Behind this belt were the panzer and Italian armored divisions, positioned so that they could provide fire support and be able to move quickly to any sector under threat. One problem, though, was that most of the mines were antitank, to which troops on their feet were impervious in that their weight was too light to detonate them, making them relatively easy to clear. Another critical factor was that the supply situation remained wholly unsatisfactory. Fuel remained at a premium, with less than 200 miles' worth per vehicle in-theater when the British did eventually attack. Ammunition stocks, too, were low.

As for the British, Montgomery began planning his attack as soon as the Alam Halfa battle ended. He issued his written plan on September 14. In essence, he intended to punch a hole in the northern part of Panzer Army Africa's defenses using XXX Corps, with five infantry divisions supported by a brigade of infantry tanks. They would create two corridors through the minefields. The two armored divisions making up X Corps would pass down these corridors to deal with an expected tank counterattack and then break out. The southern part of the front was the responsibility of XIII Corps, which was to make a diversionary attack designed to pin down Axis mobile reserves. This corps was reinforced by the deployment of dummy tanks and other vehicles, which it was hoped that Axis air reconnaissance would spot. Unlike Panzer Army Africa, the Eighth Army's logistics were in very good shape.

From October 10 onward the Axis were expecting an attack. It came in the night of October 23–24 and was preceded by a barrage fired by 456 guns, the largest of the desert war, although small compared to the barrages of 1914–18. British engineer mine-clearing parties and infantry then began to advance. Because of the ammunition shortage Stumme forbade his guns from replying to the opening barrage by firing on the likely British assembly areas, which Rommel considered a mistake.[5] The barrage itself cut communications, which were largely reliant on wire, and destroyed a number of heavy weapons. By daylight the British had established the southern corridor and seized the vital Miteiriya Ridge. The armored division, which was now supposed to pass through, did not do so, not thinking that its time had come. The northern corridor had not progressed so well, mainly because there were German troops in this sector. Back at Panzer Army headquarters Stumme, having little idea of what was happening because of the severed communications, decided to go forward and see for himself. Unlike Rommel, and against Westphal's advice, he refused to take an escort vehicle and signals truck with him and set off for headquarters of the 164th Light Division with just one staff officer. They never arrived.

Far away in Austria Rommel was in a sanatorium on Semmering Mountain, close to Wiener Neustadt. He had been there for some three weeks, not long enough to restore him to full health, when at 3:00 P.M. on October 24 he received a telephone call from Field Marshal Wilhelm Keitel. The OKW chief of staff told him of the attack and stated that Stumme was missing. He then went on to ask Rommel whether he was fit enough to return to North Africa and reassume command. Rommel said that he was, and Keitel said that he would let him know in due course. Rommel spent the next few hours "in a state of acute anxiety." Hitler then personally phoned and said that Stumme was still missing and asked Rommel whether he would be prepared to fly out immediately. Accordingly, Rommel ordered an aircraft for 7:00 A.M. next morning and returned home to Weiner Neustadt. On his arrival there Hitler phoned again and confirmed that he was to go back to Africa. So Rommel did: "I knew there were no more laurels to be earned in Africa, for I had been told in the reports I have received from my officers that supplies had fallen far short of my minimum demands."[6] He landed in Rome midmorning on October 25 and was met by Rintelen, who had grave news. Stumme was still missing and casualties were heavy. Worse, during the few weeks Rommel was away, the Italians had been unable, partly because of a lack of shipping and partly because of sinkings by the British, to provide any additional fuel. Realizing that this would severely limit his options, Rommel flew on to North Africa with a heavy heart.

He arrived back at his headquarters that evening and learned that Stumme, or at least his body, had been found. His car had been ambushed and the officer accompanying him killed. The driver had spun the car round, and Stumme jumped out and hung on as the car raced for safety. It seems that he then suffered a heart attack and fell off. Curiously, the driver stated that he had been unaware of this.

Tactically, the fuel problem dominated all; without it, the mobile forces could do no more than carry out limited local counterattacks. The 15th Panzer Division had carried out a number of these, but largely as a result of artillery fire and attacks by the Desert Air Force, which supported the Eighth Army, its strength had fallen to 31 fit tanks from the 119 that it had had at the start of the attack. Rommel saw the aim of the next few days as driving the British out of the lodgment they had made in his main defensive position. There was, however, no relaxation in the pressure that Montgomery was applying. During the night of October 25–26 XXX Corps continued its attacks and managed to secure Hill 28, located one mile northwest of Miteiriya Ridge and known by the British as Kidney Ridge. The next day was marked by a series of desperate counterattacks as the Axis forces tried to drive the British off this feature. They failed but at least prevented any farther British advance westward.

Montgomery now changed the direction of the XXX Corps assault to the northwest, toward the coast. It would, however, take a couple of days to organize, but the British maintained local pressure. The Axis supply situation continued to deteriorate, with a tanker being bombed and sunk outside Tobruk. It was for this reason that the Italian ships that got through were landing most of the supplies at Benghazi, meaning, of course, added transit time before they arrived at the front. Rommel ideally wanted to mass his armor and launch a major counterattack, but the fuel shortage did not allow this, and hence piecemeal assaults were all that he could do. As before, he was constantly going up to the battlefield to see for himself what was happening. By October 28 all the Axis armor was deployed in the north, and it was becoming a question of just how much longer that Panzer Army Africa could hold on. Rommel wrote to Lucie that day: "Who knows whether I'll have the chance to sit down and write in peace in the next few days, or ever again. . . . The battle is raging. Perhaps we will still manage to stick it out, in spite of all that's against us—but it may go wrong, and that would have very grave consequences for the whole course of the war."[7] While he was publicly declaring that there would be no retreat, in private he began to draw up a plan for withdrawing to Fuqa, sixty miles to the west. He discussed this with Westphal on the afternoon of October 29 and also began to move nonessential parts of his army back even farther, to Mersa Matruh.

Montgomery's attempt to reach the coast and cut off the northern part of Panzer Army Africa narrowly failed. He therefore recast his plan. With the Axis armor now all in the north, XXX Corps would once more attack westward while X Corps kept the Axis tanks tied down to the northwest. There was another slight lull, but the pounding of Panzer Army Africa continued. One slight consolation for Rommel was that the Luftwaffe was now flying in some fuel, although not nearly enough to fully meet his requirements. On October 30 he was able to report to Lucie that the situation was "a little quieter. I've had some sleep, am in good spirits and hope to pull it off even yet."[8] The thirty-first brought another crisis when British tanks actually reached the coast road. Rommel dashed up there himself and organized a counterattack that drove the British back across the railway line that ran south of and parallel to the coast road. It was another crisis averted, but when Rommel totted up the figures, it was clear that British numerical superiority in men, tanks, and guns was growing and that

Panzer Army Africa was being ground down. Merely a thin crust remained of its once formidable defenses.

Montgomery's new major assault, code-named Supercharge, was launched in the early hours of November 2. The New Zealand Division led the way from Kidney Ridge. Rommel was determined to snuff out this attack and to do so organized an attack from three directions—the 21st Panzer in the north and the 15th Panzer, supported by what remained of the two Italian armored divisions (Littorio, which had arrived from Italy in July, and Ariete), from the west and southwest. Ultra forewarned Montgomery of the attack, and the New Zealanders were informed. The battle that followed resulted in heavy casualties on both sides, but it was the Panzer Army Africa that came off worst. While its resistance did prevent a complete breakthrough, it was left by evening with just thirty-five German and twenty Italian tanks which were still battleworthy, and both of the two Italian armored divisions were in considerable disarray. Given his supply situation, the dominance of the Desert Air Force, and Montgomery's overwhelming numerical superiority, Rommel realized that the time had come to withdraw if he was to stand any chance of saving his army. Accordingly, he began to withdraw his divisions in the southern part of the line to the position he had occupied prior to the attack at Alam Halfa. In the north his remaining armor and the 90th Light Division would begin to pull back more slowly so as to enable as much as possible of his infantry force to get away. The orders he gave began with the statement "Under superior enemy pressure, the Army is preparing to withdraw, step by step, still fighting."[9] It was a question now of squaring Rommel's decision with the wishes of his superiors.

In a signal that Rommel sent to OKW on the afternoon of November 2 he warned that Panzer Army Africa was now in no fit state to ward off another British attempt at a breakthrough and that "the gradual destruction of the Army must therefore be assumed to be inevitable, despite the heroic resistance and exemplary spirit of the troops."[10] The signal made no mention of any withdrawal, and it was Commando Supremo in Rome that appears to have first heard about Rommel's intention to withdraw; the source was Cavallero's liaison officer with Rommel. Cavallero's reaction was one of anger, since he apparently believed that Rommel had 250 tanks and sufficient supplies. Accordingly, on November 3 he signaled Rommel that Mussolini considered it essential that he should hold on to his present positions and assured him that additional supplies were being sent to him. At the time, Hitler was at Rastenburg in East Prussia, ensconced in the Wolf's Lair headquarters he used for directing operations on the Eastern Front. At 8:30 A.M. he was informed that Rommel's midnight situation report included the statement that he was withdrawing his infantry divisions. This was followed by his morning report, which stated that the withdrawal was going according to plan. A furious Hitler drafted a message to be sent to Rommel. It stated that the whole German nation was watching him and had faith in him and his troops. "In your situation there can be no thought but to persevere, to yield not one yard, and to hurl every gun and every fighting man available into the battle." Rommel would receive considerable Luftwaffe reinforcements and Mussolini and his staff were doing their utmost to meet his supply demands. He ended the signal: "To your troops therefore you can only offer one path—Victory or Death."[11]

Rommel spent the morning of November 3 in the coast road area watching the withdrawal. Luckily for him, the British did not take immediate advantage of the situation. He returned to Panzer Army headquarters for lunch, and during it one of his staff brought in Hitler's signal. It threw Rommel into a turmoil. The withdrawal was now virtually a fait accompli, but no one disobeyed a Hitler order, not least he who owed so much to his Führer and had sworn an oath of loyalty to him. He drafted a number of signals in reply, but none were sent. He then spoke to Wilhelm von Thoma, the DAK commander. Much hinged on his extricating the Axis formations in the north since it was his tanks which would provide the rearguard. Thoma stated that he had a mere forty-one tanks left. Rommel told him that he must fight to the utmost—and read out Hitler's order. Thoma could see the madness in it and managed to get Rommel's agreement to minor withdrawals. After giving similar orders to the other formations, Rommel signaled OKW that his German contingent had suffered up to 50 percent casualties, he had only twenty-four Germans tanks still running, and the Italian armored divisions were, to all intents and purposes, destroyed. Then, believing that a dedicated Nazi Party member might make more impact than a staff officer, he dispatched the faithful Berndt to Rastenburg to plead with Hitler in person to rescind his order. He also wrote a letter to Lucie, which Berndt took with him. He wrote: "I can no longer, or scarcely any longer, believe in its successful outcome. . . . What will become of us is in God's hands."[12] Enclosed with it was some Italian currency.

The next morning at 8:00 A.M. the British began their breakout attack. The northern ten miles of what remained of the German defenses was held by the remnants of the DAK and the 90th Light Division. Below them was the Italian armored corps, and south of it the Italian X Corps. The main blow came against the DAK, which hung on grimly. Rommel was still undecided whether to obey Hitler's order to the letter or to withdraw and save his army. Kesselring came to see him, and Rommel blamed the Luftwaffe for sending back overly optimistic reports on the situation. Kesselring said that Hitler had not based his order on these, but on his experience of the Eastern Front. Rommel retorted that Hitler could not apply Russia to Africa and that he should have left the decision to Rommel. Thereupon Kesselring said that Rommel, as the man on the spot, should do what he thought best. Clearly he was guarding his back and absolving himself from any responsibility for Rommel's disobeying Hitler's order. Rommel himself was still not sure what to do; to disobey a direct order from the commander-in-chief of the German Armed Forces was a very grave step to take. On Kesselring's advice, he sent a signal to Hitler stating that his army had been decimated and he could not hold on to his present line. If any of North Africa was to be retained, he had to be allowed to carry out a fighting withdrawal. He therefore went to visit the DAK to see exactly what was happening. He noted that it was the Italians in the south who were now suffering and that part of their line had been broken. The DAK was holding on, although its headquarters combat unit, Thoma with it, was under heavy attack. Indeed, it was shortly afterward overrun and the DAK commander was captured. Montgomery had him to dinner and to stay the night. Bayerlein, the chief of staff, managed to get away on foot and assumed command of the DAK. Rommel now heard that the British had broken through the Italians. He finally accepted that he could not see his army needlessly destroyed, and at 3:00 P.M. he gave orders for the DAK to withdraw, initially to the southwest of El Daba. That evening Hitler sent a reply that reached Rommel the following day: "In view of the way things have gone I approve your request."[13]

Rommel faced one of those dilemmas that commanders in the field fear most—receipt of an order from a superior far away that reflects little of the true situation on the ground and, if carried out, will lead to disaster. For someone like him, who was used to quick decision making, it was out of character to agonize for so long, although he had done the same at Alam Halfa. Yet, apart from the oath he had sworn to Hitler, he was well aware that the German dictator could be ruthless toward anyone who disobeyed him. Nowadays, at least in the Western democracies, the most severe penalty that a commander can receive for disobeying what he considers to be unreasonable orders is to be removed from command. A commander of integrity will be prepared to risk this, especially if his troops are being placed in unacceptable danger. In the case of Rommel the situation was more difficult, mainly because of the oath he had sworn. Be that as it may, Hitler's refusal to give permission for Rommel to withdraw from El Alamein marked the beginning of the split between the two men, although it would take some time to widen.

Panzer Army Africa suffered 15,000 men killed and wounded and a further 7,000 made prisoner, and it lost 400 tanks and 1,000 artillery and antitank guns during the Second Battle of El Alamein. During the first few days of the British pursuit, another 23,000 prisoners fell into their hands, the majority of them Italian infantry who had not been able to get away because they lacked transport. Yet, in spite of the British armor's attempts to cut him off through a series of shallow hooks, Rommel did manage to get the remnants away.

His hopes of holding at Fuqa were quickly dashed by another British hook, and so he withdrew to Mersa Matruh. Rain arriving on the night of November 6 slowed the British and provided Rommel with a slight breathing space at Mersa Matruh. There he took stock of the situation. He had just twelve tanks left. The DAK mustered no more than a regiment's worth of men, and the 90th and 164th Light Divisions were in a similar situation, as was the Ramcke Parachute Brigade. The coast road, the main avenue of escape, was clogged with traffic, and the fuel situation was precarious, to say the least. While thirty-five new tanks were due to arrive at Benghazi on November 8, Rommel was told that it would take many days for them to be delivered to him. It was clear that he would have to pull right back.

On that same day, November 6, Rommel was visited by an emissary from Cavallero. He brought a message from Commando Supremo demanding that Rommel hold the frontier. Rommel knew this to be impossible and said so. Two days later the retreat resumed. Rommel now had a new chief engineer officer, the energetic Karl Bülowius. His men, with the 164th Light Division, which provided the rearguard, now set about creating obstacles and minefields, real and dummy, as well as booby traps, anything to slow the British advance. Berndt also returned from Germany with fresh orders from Hitler. Rommel was to establish a new front in Africa, but it was up to him where it should be. He also promised to bring Panzer Army Africa up to full strength.

Things were starting to look up again, but they were immediately dampened by news of the Anglo-American landings in French North Africa, some 2,000 miles in Rommel's rear. This worried him in two ways. First, it presented a new threat, albeit small, to Panzer Army Africa. Rommel also feared that it might jeopardize the reinforcements and supplies that Hitler had promised him. He asked Kesselring and Cavallero to come and visit him so that a new strategy for the war in Africa could be agreed. His request was ignored. With no one guaranteeing to him that Tunisia would be held, Rommel sent Berndt back to Germany to see Hitler once more with a proposal for evacuating his army from Libya. Berndt had his audience in Munich on November 12. Hitler was irritable and told Berndt that Rommel was not to concern himself with Tunisia and to assume that it would be held (German reinforcements had already begun to fly in). There was to be no question of Panzer

Army Africa being evacuated. It was to establish a position at Mersa Brega and be prepared to launch a counteroffensive. The reinforcements and supplies he needed would be delivered to Tripoli.

Meanwhile, the withdrawal continued. Rommel had intended to halt temporarily at Tobruk so as to retrieve 10,000 tons of matériel there. He had been making continual requests for just fuel to be flown in, but they had been ignored. He did receive 1,100 reinforcements in this way, but they could not be properly equipped for battle and had no transport, so they merely became another strain on his already limited resources. There were also frequent demands from Rome to buy as much time as possible during the retreat, but as Rommel wrote, "The speed of the retreat was now dictated solely by the enemy and our petrol situation."[14] On November 13 the first elements of Panzer Army Africa reached Mersa Brega, but the main body was still withdrawing from Tobruk. Next day Rommel wrote to Lucie: "We have to be grateful for every day that the enemy does not close on us. How far we shall get I cannot say. It all depends on the petrol, which has yet to be flown across to us."[15] The Luftwaffe was, in fact, flying in fuel, but nowhere close to Rommel's demand of 250 tons per day. He again asked Cavallero, who was in Libya, to come and see him, but instead the Italian chief of staff sent the German air attaché to Rome with orders for Rommel to delay at least another week in Cyrenaica and to hold the Mersa Brega Line at all costs.

Rommel later revealed his bitterness toward Cavallero for his consistent failures to keep his army properly supplied. He saw him as belonging to "to the type of officer of the intellectually fairly well qualified, but weak-willed office-chair soldier. The organization of supplies, the command of men, anything in any way constructive requires more than intellect;

it requires energy and drive and an unrelenting will to serve the cause, regardless of one's personal interests."[16] The Cavallero type tended to look down on the field commander who lacked formal staff training or academic qualifications, as Rommel did, and he was clearly intensely irritated by it. The problem of the divide between the professional staff officer and the fighting soldier has been one which all armies have suffered. Nowadays it is much less severe, since most armies have a policy of ensuring that officers alternate service with troops with staff appointments, making them better equipped to appreciate the perspective of each, and so friction between the two is minimized.

Rommel's frustration increased when he learned that several ships loaded with fuel had been turned back before reaching Benghazi and that a tanker had left the port with fuel still on board. The reason for this dereliction was that the Italian logistics staff had set in motion the destruction of dumps and facilities in the port. Luckily, more rain arrived. It produced some flooding in the Msus area and foiled a British attempt to use the route through the base of the Cyrenaican bulge. Rommel evacuated Benghazi on November 19, and on the same day the DAK arrived at Mersa el Brega. Italian infantry divisions were occupying it and working hard to improve the defenses. The British made no attempt to rush the position. Montgomery was well aware that his supply lines were now very overstretched and wanted to reopen the port of Benghazi before advancing farther. Yet, as with almost everywhere else in the desert, the Mersa Brega position could be easily outflanked, although an attacking force needed to go some way south in order to do so. Rommel appreciated this only too well and was aware that his supply line back to Tripoli was also long. His current shortage of tanks and fuel also meant that he lacked the mobile forces to successfully counter any outflanking move and was certain that Montgomery could build up his forces in western Cyrenaica more quickly than the Axis forces. He also knew that the Allied forces were beginning to advance into Tunisia. It therefore seemed to him that staying put would lead to disaster. He sent General Guiseppe de Stefanis, commander of the Italian armored corps and one of the few Italian officers for whom Rommel had much regard, to Rome to explain to Mussolini and Cavallero how things stood with Panzer Army Africa and that it would be fatal to fight at Mersa Brega. While de Stefanis was away, Rommel received a signal from Hitler reiterating that he must hold where he was and again promising that he would receive the necessary matériel support. It also reminded him that he was subordinate to Marshal Ettore Bastico, the Italian supreme commander in North Africa, which had been the case prior to Rommel's advance into Egypt in the summer, after which he had been answerable direct to Commando Supremo in Rome and OKW.

Rommel met Bastico on November 22. He explained his reasons for wanting to withdraw farther and argued that there was no feasible defensive position in Tripolitania. He therefore proposed pulling back into Tunisia, where Panzer Army Africa could join up with the now assembling Fifth Panzer Army. From a position based on Gabès, 120 miles west of the border with Libya, they could strike at the Allies in western Tunisia and then turn on Montgomery, who would, in any event, need time to build up his supplies before crossing into Tunisia. Bastico was initially, and probably not surprisingly, resistant to Rommel's plan, but he eventually agreed to put it to Commando Supremo. Two days later Kesselring and Cavallero finally met Rommel. The meeting took place at a triumphal arch that the Italians had erected on the coast road where it crossed the Tripolitania-Cyrenaica border, and was known by the British as Marble Arch. Rather than unilaterally disobeying the order to stay put, Rommel knew that what he was proposing would affect what was happening in Tunisia and that his operations would need to be coordinated with those of Fifth Panzer Army, Only the Axis higher command could do this. Hence he had to cajole and persuade. In this instance he began by pointing out to Kesselring and Cavallero the severe supply problems his army had suffered from El Alamein onward. The German element was now reduced to the equivalent of one weak division, and the equipment of the three Italian divisions actually holding the line was in such a poor state that they were not capable of combat. Withdrawal was therefore the only answer, but when he stated that the whole of Tripolitania would have to be evacuated the two men blanched. On November 26 Kesselring and Cavallero responded to Rommel's demand. While Kesselring ordered him to detach troops to protect Tripoli, Cavallero stated Mussolini was demanding that not only was the present position to be held at all costs but that Rommel should attack the British as soon as possible. Should they attack, any decision to withdraw would rest with Bastico and not Rommel. There was only one thing for it: Rommel would have to see Hitler in person.

Without requesting Bastico's permission, Rommel immediately flew off to Germany accompanied by Berndt. After calling in briefly to see Lucie, he arrived at the Wolf's Lair at Rastenburg in the afternoon of November 28. He met Keitel and Alfred Jodl, his deputy. They asked him what he was doing there and he was then ushered in to see Hitler. The latter first asked Rommel why he had left his command without permission. Rommel immediately launched into an account of his problems, but then became aware that Hitler had other things on his mind. The German Sixth Army, under Rommel's old acquaintance Friedrich Paulus, was trapped at Stalingrad, and efforts were now being made to rescue it. Hitler therefore did not take kindly to an account of the difficulties in what was a minor theater of war compared to the Eastern Front. When Rommel then stated that North Africa should be evacuated, Hitler became furious. The repercussions for Italy would be very grave. Mussolini could be overthrown, which would make Italy's status as an Axis power uncertain. Hitler declared that Rommel would be given all the weapons he wanted, and more. Kesselring would organize air cover for his supply convoys. Hitler concluded by stating that he would send Mussolini a telegram and that Rommel was to accompany Hermann Göring on a visit to Rome to arrange matters. That evening, accompanied by the faithful Berndt, Rommel boarded Göring's state train, which stopped briefly at Munich to pick up Lucie so that she could spend some precious time with her husband. Rommel was quickly angered by Göring's attitude and became convinced that the head of the Luftwaffe and deputy führer wanted to take control of Africa himself.

Rommel therefore decided to employ Berndt's talents to win Göring round. His persuasiveness proved highly successful, and Göring became enthusiastic about the idea of a joint Fifth Panzer Army and Panzer Army Africa offensive into Morocco and Algeria. Berndt also suggested that Rommel's retreat from El Alamein could be spun as an intentional move to tackle the Allied forces in Tunisia. On the party's arrival in Rome Kesselring ridiculed the idea, especially since the farther Rommel withdrew, the greater danger the Luftwaffe's bases in the Mediterranean would be in because of the shortened range for Allied aircraft.

During the subsequent meetings with Mussolini and his generals, the argument continued. Eventually Mussolini decided on a compromise. Rommel would be allowed to withdraw from Mersa Brega, but only when Montgomery was on the point of attacking him. He would not be allowed to pull back into Tunisia, but only to Buerat, 200 miles east of Tripoli. This fell far short of Rommel's demand for an immediate withdrawal from Tripolitania, but it was better than being ordered to stay put.

Worse was to follow. Göring publicly insulted Rommel at a lunch held at the end of the conference. Then at a further meeting over supply matters it became clear that much of the matériel that had been earmarked for Rommel had actually been diverted to Tunisia. Panzer Army Africa would have to survive on the limited resources it currently possessed.

Rommel landed back in Libya early on December 2. Lieutenant Ambruster, Rommel's interpreter, noted in his diary: "CinC seems to have been torn off a strip by the Führer."[17] Rommel was certainly downcast. As he wrote to Lucie: "I don't feel at all well. My nerves are shot to pieces."[18] Göring had also told Hitler that in his estimation Rommel was no longer fit. Nevertheless there was much work to be done. The withdrawal had to be finalized, and Rommel needed to examine the Buerat position. He also wanted to obtain as much fuel as he could so that the withdrawal could take place. By December 6 he had enough for one of the Italian infantry divisions to pull back. Sensing that the British were making their final preparations for an attack and with Bastico's agreement, this division departed that night. In spite of orders that it should be done without lights, its trucks drove out with headlights glaring. The British did not appear to notice. This was repeated on subsequent nights, and by December 11 all but the armor had got away, putting Rommel in a more cheerful frame of mind. That night the British artillery began to bombard the Mersa Brega defenses as the outflanking force began its approach march. It was time for the DAK and what was left of the Italian tanks to depart. It was successfully done, and by dawn the position was empty of Axis troops. As Rommel later noted, the British made a cardinal mistake in not allowing the outflanking force to get close to the coast road before the artillery barrage opened.

Rommel had got away, but his tanks only had enough fuel to take them some thirty miles, while Buerat lay over 200 miles away. Their crews just had to hope that more would become available. During the next few days this hand-to-mouth existence continued. In some instances the fuel had to be drained from some tanks to give others enough to fight a mobile action. The Desert Air Force also continued to harass the Axis forces. Skillful actions by the rearguards saved the day on more than once occasion and enabled Panzer Army Africa to go firm on the Buerat Line by December 26, having withdraw some 210 miles in eleven days. Rommel knew from the start that it was a totally unsatisfactory position because it could be outflanked. His intention was therefore to hold it long enough to bring the British to a halt and then to continue the withdrawal, halting next on the line Tarhuna-Homs. He intended to use the same technique of pulling back the Italian infantry first. The supply situation was still grim—the British had recently sunk nine out of ten tankers sent to Rommel—and the supply line to Tripoli was still relatively long. Bastico fully agreed with Rommel and they submitted a joint estimate of the situation to Commando Supremo. The response came in the form of an order from Mussolini that Panzer Army Africa was to resist "to the uttermost" on the Buerat Line. Rommel's response was to ask Cavallero what should happen if the British did not engage the line directly but bypassed it. His reply was that on no account were Italian troops to be sacrificed as they had been during the retreat from El Alamein. A furious Rommel immediately sent a message to Bastico stating that he could not defend Buerat to the "uttermost" and ensure that the Italian infantry got away safely. Bastico gave no clear-cut answer, but Rommel was sympathetic to his position. After all, Bastico was also governor of Libya and therefore could not display much enthusiasm for surrendering the whole colony.

Luckily for Rommel and Bastico, Montgomery chose to halt in front of Buerat, rather than immediately outflank it, so that his supplies could once more catch up. While this pause appeared very cautious, he was very conscious from the previous desert campaigns of what could happen if supply lines became overextended. It was a specter that haunted the coalition logisticians in both the 1991 and 2003 wars against Iraq, given the rapid pace of the advances on each occasion. Generals Norman Schwarzkopf and Tommy Franks were also well aware of this in their respective planning, but they had more time than Rommel or Montgomery to prepare for this eventuality. Unlike in Rommel's case during the advance to El Alamein, they were also totally in command and did not have to depend largely on a superior authority of a different nationality for a reliable flow of supplies. Consequently, they were able to stockpile supplies prior to launching their attacks and ensure that they had sufficient transport, both air and ground, to deliver them. As a result fuel tanks did not run dry, and weapon systems were not immobilized through lack of ammunition.

Montgomery's pause at Buerat—he did not intend to advance further west until mid-January—gave Rommel another opportunity to plead his case. On December 31 he had another meeting with Bastico. Commando Supremo had finally weakened, albeit slightly, and agreed that there could be a withdrawal from Buerat, but only after it was clear that the destruction of Panzer Army Africa looked imminent. Thereafter Rommel was expected to fight on in Tripolitania for at least two months before withdrawing into Tunisia so as to allow the total destruction of the port to be prepared. Rommel told Bastico that it would take at least eight days to get the Italian infantry back to Homs. The supply situation had by now improved, with Tunis the main entry port. Better food also improved the health and morale of the army. Fuel still remained short, however, and Rommel was still determined to withdraw from the Buerat Line before he was attacked. He and Bastico had another meeting with Kesselring and Cavallero on January 6. Cavallero said that Commando Supremo had reluctantly agreed that Tripolitania should no longer be held since the concern now was Tunis, the last significant supply port held by the Axis in North Africa. It had been under threat from the Allied forces in western Tunisia since the end of November, and they had at one point got to within twenty miles of Tunis before being turned back by Fifth Panzer Army. To this end Bastico asked Rommel if he would send one of his divisions to Tunisia. Rommel agreed with alacrity, nominating the 21th Panzer Division, but stated that it must leave behind all its equipment and be reequipped in Tunisia. Kesselring, who had consistently opposed Rommel's endless withdrawals and, indeed, wanted him to counterattack the British at Buerat, strongly disagreed. Berndt was dispatched to Rastenburg once more and Hitler came down on Rommel's side, believing Tunisia to now be more important than Tripolitania. There was, however, a proviso to the agreement to withdraw. Panzer Army Africa was still expected to defend Tripoli for at least six weeks.

Axis radio intelligence established that the British intended to attack on January 15, and so they did. Rommel withdrew in contact, both the 15th Panzer and the 90th Light Divisions doing well to ward off British blows. Once more, though, the tension was getting to Rommel: " . . . the nervous strain is particularly severe just now and I have to keep a real grip on myself," he wrote to Lucie.[19] Any thoughts of holding the Tarhuna-Homs Line were soon dispelled. The British were moving rapidly and in superior force. Fuel, too, was again in short supply. Rommel warned Bastico of this and that the British could arrive in front of Tripoli as early as January 20. He began to send his Italian infantry away first, as usual, but hoped to buy some time on the Tarhuna-Homs Line, especially since the terrain to the south was hilly and broken and made it relatively more difficult to outflank than other positions he had held. The British attacked again on January 19, concentrating on the Tarhuna area and enabling Rommel to continue the withdrawal of his troops around Homs in the north. It then became clear that the British tactic was to pin down the defenses around Tarhuna while they carried out an outflanking move. Rommel continued to hold, while preparing to withdraw the rest of his army. Early on January 20, with demolitions already taking place in Tripoli, he received a signal from Rome stating that Rommel had disobeyed Mussolini's orders and had to remain where he was for at least three weeks so that the defenses in Tunisia, which were based on the French-built Mareth Line, could be strengthened. Rommel was once more furious with those so far away from and out of touch with the true situation on the ground. He gave Cavallero a stark choice. Tripoli could be held for a few days and the army lost, or given up and the army kept intact to fight another day in Tunisia. Rommel now obtained information that the British outflanking move was more ambitious than he had thought and its objective was a point thirty miles west of Tripoli. Consequently, on January 22 he gave orders for the evacuation of both the Tarhuna position and Tripoli. The army moved to the west of the city and the British entered it in triumph next day. On January 25 Panzer Army Africa crossed the border into Tunisia.

In Rome there was fury, and on January 26, 1943, Rommel received a signal relieving him of command on the grounds of ill health once his army arrived within the Mareth Line. Rommel admitted in a letter to Lucie that his health was not too good: "Severe headaches and overstrained nerves, on top of the circulation trouble allow me no rest." He was certain, though, that his health was not the reason for his dismissal, but rather it was "principally that of [Italian] prestige."[20] His was not the only head to roll. Bastico was also sacked, about which Rommel was sorry, and Cavallero also went, to Rommel's delight. Rommel's army was also redesignated the First Italian Army, and an Italian was nominated to command it.

In the meantime Rommel still had much to do before his successor arrived. An examination of the Mareth Line revealed a vulnerability; it, too, could be outflanked. The French had carried out an experiment using trucks in 1938 and concluded from it that it was not possible to get round its southern flank (the other flank rested on the sea), but Rommel was convinced—rightly as it turned out—that Montgomery's Eighth Army was capable of achieving this. His mobile forces needed to be deployed to counter this eventuality, but they also were expected to deploy to Gafsa at the southern end of the Eastern Dorsale, Tunisia's mountainous spine, to guard against the British First Army in western Tunisia. Rommel therefore advocated withdrawing forty miles north to Wadi Akarit, which could only be attacked frontally. His proposal was ignored, so Panzer Army Africa positioned itself in the Mareth Line. Then, on February 2, Giovanni Messe, Rommel's designated successor, came to have lunch with him. Rommel got on well with him but decided that he was going to hold on to his command until he was actually pushed. The reason was a plan that had been hatched by Kesselring.

Kesselring had estimated that it would be some time before Montgomery made an advance on the Mareth Line since he needed to get Tripoli fully operational as a port and to reorganize his forces. In the West the British First Army was occupying a very long front of some 350 miles, but it was thinly held, with the British V Corps in the north, the French XIX Corps in the center, and U.S. II Corps in the south. Even so, the Fifth Panzer Army under Hans-Jürgen von Arnim was still occupying a relatively narrow part of the country, with Tunis at its base. Kesselring therefore conceived the mounting of a series of spoiling attacks in the west, both to keep the Allies unbalanced and to push them back. This was approved by both OKW and Commando Supremo. Arnim led the way when on January 30 he sent three Italian divisions and the reequipped 21st Panzer Division against the French-held Faid Pass, which provided the route to Tunisia's coastal plain through the center of the Eastern Dorsale. This was successful, and the French were driven back. Rommel himself was concerned over Gafsa, which lay in the American sector. A thrust through here would split the two Axis armies. He therefore proposed an attack, but he did not wish to commit the 15th Panzer Division in case Montgomery began to move and so asked for the use of some of Arnim's forces. Arnim himself wanted to exploit his success at Faid and wished to move on to Sidi Bou Zid, to strengthen his hold on the Eastern Dorsale. He was therefore unwilling to hand troops over to Rommel. Matters were not helped by the fact that there was mutual antipathy between the two men. Kesselring chaired a meeting between the two on February 9, and it was agreed that Arnim would attack on February 12 and Rommel two days later. The object was not so much to gain territory as to inflict casualties on the relatively unbloodied Americans. Kesselring apparently asked Rommel's doctor whether he was fit enough to conduct such an operation, and his reply was that Rommel should leave Africa on about February 20. Kesselring therefore agreed to give Rommel "this one last chance of glory."[21]

The day of Arnim's attack marked the second anniversary of Rommel's arrival in Africa. The band of the 8th Panzer Regiment serenaded him in the morning, and the few officers of the DAK who had been with him since the start, nineteen in all, joined him for a small celebration. Arnim's attack went well. Sidi Bou Zid was held by elements of the U.S. 1st Armored Division. They were pushed out of there, and on February 17 Sbeitla, twenty-five miles to the northwest, was also in Arnim's hands. Rommel himself had organized an ad hoc battle group from what was left of the DAK for his attack on Gafsa. It arrived there as night fell on February 15 to find the town deserted. The Americans had withdrawn in reaction to Arnim's attack farther north. Rommel himself dashed up there next morning and noted abandoned equipment and other evidence of a hurried American departure. It seemed as if they were falling back on Tebessa, beyond the border with Algeria. Rommel, seeming to forget his ailments, saw that if he could seize Tebessa, an important communications center with an airfield, he would strike the Allies a grievous blow. Arnim did not agree, and so Rommel approached Kesselring, hoping that the Commander-in-Chief South's perpetual optimism would work in Rommel's favor. He got Kesselring to agree and obtained approval from Commando Supremo, but rather than striking directly into the Allied rear area, which Tebessa represented, it was laid down that Thala, thirty miles northwest of Tebessa, was to be the initial objective. It was thus a much shallower operation than Rommel had in mind. He was, however, given the 10th and 21st Panzer Divisions.

The operation began on February 19. The DAK battle group had already reached Feriana, forty miles north of Gafsa by the time the attack started and now made for the Kasserine Pass, twenty miles to the northeast. Simultaneously, the 10th Panzer Division set out from Sbeitla for the pass, and part of the 21st Panzer drove north to Sbiba, but they were repulsed by a combined Anglo-American force. Kasserine Pass, which was held by the Americans, was secured by the afternoon of the next day. While elements of the Italian Centauro armored division began to advance toward Tebessa, the remainder of the force pressed on north to Thala. A British armored brigade had been hastily deployed to protect it and managed to hold up Rommel's advance throughout February 21. Reinforced overnight by U.S. artillery transported from Morocco, the defenders the following morning fired a devastating barrage on the Germans as they were forming up for another attack and caused heavy casualties. Rommel concluded that the defenses at Thala had now become too strong and ordered the attack to be halted. Kesselring then visited, and the two men agreed that the attack should be closed down and the Axis forces then gradually begin to withdraw. At this same meeting Kesselring also said that the time had come to appoint a commander to control both Fifth Panzer and First Italian Armies, and he wanted Rommel to assume command of the newly formed Army Group Africa. Rommel, knowing that Arnim had already been earmarked for the post and, in any event, personally fed up with dealing with Commando Supremo, declined. Kesselring again consulted with Rommel's doctor, who said that he could remain for another month but after that must return to Germany for a cure. This decided Kesselring.

The next morning, February 23, Rommel was formally notified of his new appointment, with Messe confirmed as commander of the First Italian Army. It was in many ways an extraordinary decision on Kesselring's part: appointing a man who was not fully fit and who would have to leave the theater within a short time in place of another man who had already been earmarked for the post makes little sense. The only explanation is Kesselring's optimism that perhaps Rommel could conjure up some of his old magic. The recent Kasserine operation had shown glimmers of the old Rommel, and so now in a position where he could coordinate operations throughout Tunisia, maybe he could restore Axis fortunes. On the other hand, Rommel's aide claimed to have arranged the promotion as a means of restoring Rommel's shaky mental health. In a letter to Lucie Berndt wrote: "I fixed it to strengthen his belief that—even after our long retreat—people still have faith in him. He himself had begun to believe the opposite."[22]

Whatever did bring about Rommel's elevation, he found that he had no properly constituted headquarters. He also quickly became aware that he was being bypassed. Arnim and Messe continued to deal directly with Commando Supremo, and Kesselring also conferred with the latter on Tunisian matters without bringing Rommel into the picture. Nevertheless, he did his best. His first task was to confer with the chief of operations at the headquarters of Fifth Panzer Army over future operations and was told of a projected attack to destroy Allied forces in the Medjez el Bab area, forty miles west of Tunis. Rommel approved the plan, except for the intention to withdraw immediately after the attack. He wanted the captured ground to be retained. That evening of February 24 he received a request from Kesselring to halt the withdrawal of the 10th Panzer Division from Kasserine; Arnim wanted it to cooperate in an attack on Beja, twenty-four miles west of Medjez. It was the first that Rommel had heard of this, and it irritated him intensely that Arnim had not chosen to discuss it with him. He considered it much too ambitious an objective for the force available. In any event, the 10th Panzer Division's withdrawal had already begun, and it was under threat of an attack that might cut it off if it stayed where it was. Arnim's attack, code-named Ox Head, began on February 26. It initially took the British by surprise, but they soon recovered. The fighting went on for some three weeks and did provide some territorial gains, but it halted well short of Beja.

Rommel, though, had now turned his eyes eastward. The Eighth Army had begun its awaited advance into Tunisia on February 7. Ten days later it came to a halt at Medenine, twenty miles south of the Mareth Line, and began to prepare to assault it. Rommel decided that an attack before the British had organized their defenses would knock them off balance and impose a considerable delay in their attack on the Mareth Line. Commando Supremo approved the idea on February 23, but it would take some days to organize the forces for it. These were made up of the 10th, 15th, and 21st Panzer Divisions as the strike force and the 90th Light and Brescia Divisions to distract British attention from the main blow. Rommel's problem was that Montgomery had timely warning of the attack through Ultra and was able to prepare for it. In addition, Rommel was in essence making a frontal assault rather than using his characteristic tactic of outflanking and then enveloping an opponent. The attack itself began at dawn on March 6 amid thick mist. British armored cars tracked his approach, and then, once the mist lifted, the tanks were subjected to intense fire from skillfully positioned antitank guns and artillery. It was a disaster. Over fifty German tanks were destroyed at little cost to the British, and the survivors were forced to withdraw. For Rommel it was the end.

He now concluded that Tunisia was lost and that the only answer was evacuation of the Axis forces. He felt that it was time for him to leave Africa and speak personally to Hitler on the subject, as well as finally take his cure. Perhaps the last straw was a signal from OKW rejecting his request for Messe to withdraw to Enfidaville, which would have reduced Army Group Africa's defense perimeter to some one hundred miles and improved the supply situation. On March 8 he handed command over to an equally despondent Arnim, his designated deputy, for in theory, but no more, Rommel would be returning. The next day Rommel left Africa a dispirited and almost broken man. Ever since he had reached his zenith at the end of June 1942 his fortunes had declined, and he must have wondered whether his days at a fighting soldier were at an end.

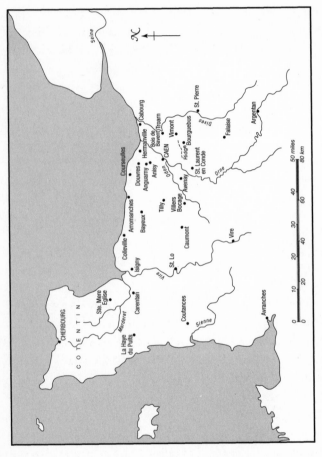

The Normandy Battlefield. Map by David Hoxley.

CHAPTER 6

Last Flourishes

ROMMEL FLEW OUT OF AFRICA AN EXHAUSTED MAN AND in a very depressed state of mind. Even though he was determined to return, he had to accept the possibility that this might not be so and he felt guilty over deserting his men. The last eight months had been a dismal time for him. There had been none of the dazzling victories that he had become used to enjoying. Instead, it had been a constant struggle, for most of the time against overwhelming odds. All he could do now was to try to save Army Group Africa from total destruction.

Rome was his first port of call and he had an audience with Mussolini, who asked him what had happened at Medenine and his views on the strength of the Mareth Line, which he had left the First Italian Army defending in Tunisia. Rommel attempted to impress upon him the need to radically shorten the defensive perimeter, but Mussolini brushed this comment aside, declaring that Tunisia had to be held at all costs, that it was simply a question of willpower. He implied that Rommel was defeatist and apparently changed his mind about presenting Rommel with the Gold Medal for Military Valor. The two did part cordially enough, though.

Rommel's next stop was to be at one of Hitler's field headquarters, in this case Vinnytsia in the Ukraine, code-named Werewolf, where the German leader was overseeing Erich von Manstein's post-Stalingrad counteroffensive. Rommel ran into Göring, who offered to take him to Vinnytsia in his special train, which Rommel declined. He arrived at Hitler's headquarters on the afternoon of March 10. He had to wait a few hours while Hitler was away visiting Manstein, but that evening was invited to take tea with him. Once more Rommel tried to impress on Hitler the seriousness of the situation in Tunisia. As they had done with Mussolini, his words on reducing the defensive perimeter and even evacuating Tunisia altogether fell on deaf ears. Rommel spent three days at Vinnytsia and did finally obtain a small concession from Hitler. He agreed that the infantry in the Mareth Line could be withdrawn to Wadi Akarit and that he would send Admiral Karl Dönitz, recently promoted to head the German navy, to Rome to impress upon Mussolini the necessity of sending adequate supplies to Tunisia. Hitler also decorated Rommel with the Diamonds to the Knight's Cross but turned down his request to return immediately to his post, telling him that he was sending him on sick leave. Instructions were given that this must be kept secret to encourage the Allies to believe that Rommel was still in Africa.

Rommel now returned to Wiener Neustadt and began his cure for his various maladies, again at the Semmering sanatorium. He had plenty to occupy himself. He had brought numerous papers with him from Africa and now set about writing up his campaigns there. These were later incorporated by Basil Liddell Hart in his book *The Rommel Papers.* The ever more gloomy news from Tunisia depressed him. Montgomery overcame the Mareth Line through a deep outflanking move, as Rommel had feared, but failed to prevent First Italian Army from getting away. He then breached the line at Wadi Akarit in early April, while pressure from the British First Army in the west mounted all along the front. Montgomery was, however, frustrated when he tried to assault Enfidaville, thus proving Rommel's estimate of its value as a defensive position to be correct. The emphasis then switched to First Army, which began a major assault toward the end of April. The Axis forces, their supply lines virtually severed through naval and air action, continued to fight as best they could, but they could not turn back the tide, and on May 7 both Tunis and Bizerta fell. The remnants of Army Group Africa then retreated to the Cape Bon Peninsula and surrendered.

On May 9, 1943, two days before the Tunisian surrender, Rommel was summoned to Berlin, but in civilian clothes so as to maintain the myth that he was still in Africa. He met a Hitler shaken by the reverse in Tunisia, which netted the Allies 240,000 prisoners of war. Coming on top of the disaster at Stalingrad it was becoming clear that the tide was fast turning in favor of the Allies. What concerned Hitler and OKW now was Italy's future, especially if the Allies invaded, and what should be done about it. In Hitler's mind the only Italian whom they could rely on was Mussolini, but if he was deposed, Italy and the Balkans, where the Italians provided the bulk of the occupation forces, would be lost. Rommel attended a number of war conferences and a plan was developed. Should Italy be invaded, Hitler intended to transfer eight panzer and four infantry divisions from the Eastern Front and move them into northern Italy under Rommel's command. To this end Rommel was to establish a skeleton army group headquarters and begin detailed planning for this eventuality. He was delighted to be in harness again, and even more so that he was able to obtain his old African comrade Alfred Gause as his chief of staff. Rommel's main concern was the Alpine passes leading into Italy. He knew perfectly well that the Italians were quite capable of closing them and that there were fortifications in place along the Italian border. Thus any German force would have to deploy very rapidly to prevent this. There were, however, two possible scenarios. The first, code-named Alaric, assumed that Italy was still in the war but required bolstering. In this event German forces would be infiltrated from Austria and Bavaria. It would, however, require careful political handling so as not to upset Italian sensitivities and throw the country into the arms of the Allies. The second option, Axis, was more drastic. Should the Italians look like defecting, their armed forces would need to be quickly disarmed. The two plans might have to be put into operation almost simultaneously and there was also the need to draw up a strategy for defending Italy. Rommel therefore had plenty to occupy himself.

Rommel continued to be frequently present at Hitler's war conferences, wherever they were held. Thus in early July he was at the Wolf's Lair in East Prussia and witnessed the opening of Operation Citadel, a major attack to pinch out the Kursk salient on the Eastern Front. After a promising start, it began to lose momentum in the face of determined Russian resistance. Then, on July 10 came the news that Anglo-American forces had landed on Sicily. It gave Hitler the excuse to close down the offensive at Kursk. Hitler's first decision was to send in more troops to join the two German divisions already on the island. Hence General Hans Hube was sent in with a panzer grenadier division and two parachute regiments. An Italian general was in overall charge, but Hitler demanded that a German be put in actual command. Rommel recommended Hube, but Göring wanted it to be a Luftwaffe officer, on the grounds that a good proportion of the force was made up of airborne troops, the province of the Luftwaffe. Hitler chose Hube, to Rommel's gratification, but two days later, on July 18, Rommel noted in his diary: "I hear the Führer has been advised not to give me command in Italy as I am adversely disposed toward the Italians. I imagine the Luftwaffe is behind this."[1] It was a blow, but Rommel was quickly given another task.

Prior to the invasion of Sicily the Allies had put into effect a number of deception plans to make the Germans believe that they would land elsewhere. One of these was Operation Mincemeat, which involved landing a dead body dressed in the uniform of a British Royal Marines officer by submarine on the Spanish coast. On his person was a letter addressed to General Sir Harold Alexander, who was commanding the Allied forces in Tunisia, stating that an invasion of Greece was being planned. This information found its way to the Germans, and Hitler became concerned, even to the extent of sending reinforcements there. Now, with the Allies steadily advancing in Sicily, Hitler was worried that an attack on Greece might be in the offing. Accordingly, on July 23 he ordered Rommel to fly to Greece and be prepared to assume command there, but also to report directly to him on the state of the country's defenses. Two days later Rommel and Gause landed at Salonika with the feeling that they were being shunted off to a backwater. That evening they had a meeting with Luftwaffe General Alexander Löhr, who was the German commander-in-chief in the Balkans. Rommel was planning to fly round the country the next day in order to get a feel for it, but late that night a telephone call from OKW changed everything.

With Sicily likely to be soon added to Italy's long list of defeats, it was becoming clear to most Italians that to preserve their country and save further casualties surrender to the Allies was the only option. Mussolini was an obstacle to this, and his leadership had proved disastrous. With the agreement of King Victor Emmanuel the Fascist Grand Council passed a vote of no confidence in Mussolini on July 25 and he was arrested. A new government under Marshal Pietro Badoglio was formed and immediately opened secret negotiations with the Allies. The call Rommel received from OKW told him that Mussolini was in protective custody and summoned him straight back to Hitler's headquarters. Rommel arrived there at noon on the twenty-sixth to find most of the Nazi hierarchy were present. The situation in Italy was still obscure, but there was no doubt that the country would surrender and that the Allies would carry out landings in its northern half. Rommel's task was to be much as it had been before, to organize the deployment of German troops in northern Italy. There was talk of putting him in charge of the forces in Sicily as well, but both Keitel and Jodl were opposed to this. According to Joseph Goebbels, "They don't want to see him getting too much power and too many troops—they are envious of him."[2] Rommel established his headquarters in a railway train in the Munich area under the cover name OKW Rehabilitation Unit Munich. Hitler specifically instructed him, Gause, and others of his staff not to set foot in either Austria or Italy for the time being. In case the Italians decided to resist in their border defenses Rommel was given two infantry divisions, some troops from a mountain training school, and three groups of powerful PzKw VI Tiger tanks from other training establishments. It was now just a matter of awaiting the word from Hitler. It was not long in coming.

On July 29 the Germans managed to eavesdrop on a telephone call between Churchill and President Franklin Roosevelt on their one-to-one transatlantic link in which Churchill spoke of the impending Italian armistice. Hitler therefore ordered Operation Alaric for the following day. The 25th Panzer Division was to be the first formation into Italy, and Rommel personally briefed the lead battalion commander. He was to be friendly to the Italians and explain that they were reinforcements being rushed to Sicily. He was only to open fire if attacked, but was to defuse all demolitions on bridges and viaducts. Although Rommel was not initially allowed to accompany his troops, as was his normal custom, he was in good humor. He believed that he would shortly take over from Kesselring as Commander-in-Chief South, especially since the latter had no control over what Rommel was doing. There were some moments of tension and indications of Italian intransigence, but in general the move of Army Group B, as Rommel's command was officially titled, went relatively smoothly. Then the Italians began to make difficulties. They tried to obstruct the road and railway movement of Rommel's forces, but he continued to take a diplomatic approach. Only when the Italians barred the way to their naval base at La Spezia did Rommel become certain that they intended to change sides. On August 11 Rommel was ordered back to the Wolf's Lair for consultations with Hitler. He thought, as Rommel did, that the Italians were going to change sides, and condemned Kesselring, the German ambassador to Rome, and Rintelen for believing otherwise. Rommel was very pleased with the confidence that Hitler was showing in him and told Jodl that Army Group B should command all the German troops in Italy, rather than just those in the north. Jodl was not so sure. Rommel was boosted further when Hitler instructed him to go to Italy and visit the Italian commanders to establish where they stood.

Rommel, accompanied by Jodl, landed at Bologna airport on the morning of August 15. Escorted by a Waffen SS battalion from Sepp Dietrich's 1st SS Panzer Division, the Leibstandarte, which was now under Army Group B, they drove to a villa outside the city to meet the Italian generals. Rommel left it to Jodl to do most of the talking. The meeting did not go well. General Mario Roatta, the Italian spokesman, was evasive in his answers to Jodl's questions. He also strongly objected to the presence of SS troops in Italy. When Jodl told him that the intention was for Rommel to command all Axis troops in northern Italy, while Kesselring did the same in the south, Roatta proposed that Rommel move his troops down to the center and south of the country. This deployment would mean, of course, that with Italian forces in the north the Germans would be cut off. Two days later General Vittorio Ambrosio wrote an angry letter to OKW demanding that Rommel leave Italy. Commando Supremo, he claimed, had brought about his removal from Tunisia, and it was entirely inappropriate for Rommel to be given a command in Italy. That same day Rommel traveled to Lake Garda, where he intended to establish his headquarters. On the same day General George S. Patton's U.S. Seventh Army entered Messina, marking the end of the Sicilian campaign. The German divisions on the island had, however, made good their escape to the Italian mainland.

Setting up his headquarters was not without difficulty, especially since the Italians refused to allow him to lay telephone cables back to Germany, but there were also other things on Rommel's mind. The Allied strategic air offensive against Germany was growing more intense, especially with the "firestorm" raids on Hamburg by RAF Bomber Command. Wiener Neustadt was close to the Messerschmitt aircraft factories, and Rommel became worried that his house might be destroyed. He therefore decided that he must move all his papers, silver, and other valuables to safety. Recalling that one of his brother officers in the Württemberg Mountain Battalion had a farm deep in the Bavarian countryside, Rommel flew to see him on August 22 and he agreed to look after the Rommel possessions. At the same time he told Lucie to begin house hunting and suggested a move to Württemberg. This was done, and Rommel once more turned his attention to Italy.

He realized that it was very possible he would find himself faced with Allied landings and thought that the port of La Spezia was the most likely objective, since the Allies could then seize the Italian ships based there. At the same time, he could well have to put Operation Axis into effect. He had come to the conclusion that the only way to defeat seaborne landings was on the beaches; hence he wanted to deploy his forces to guard the coastline, but this might mean that he did not have enough strength to disarm, and possibly fight, the Italians at the same time. For these reasons he believed that the whole of German strength in Italy should be concentrated in the north. A further reason was that it made little military sense for the Allies to land in the south of the country since this would leave them having to fight their way up the entire length of Italy. Kesselring saw it differently, through the eyes of an airman. The Allies would need fighter air cover for their landings. Support could be provided from Sicily, but even this location meant that northern Italy was beyond the effective range of Allied fighters. Besides which, the good airfields in Italy were all in the south, and if they were surrendered, the Luftwaffe would not be able to properly support the ground forces in the north. Kesselring had sent his air commander,

Wolfram von Richthofen, to see Rommel on August 17 to represent his views. While they agreed on how the Italians should be handled—with ruthlessness—they were at loggerheads over everything else. Rommel, Richthofen wrote, "lacks any overall view. Sees things only from the narrowest possible army standpoint, regardless of the strategic situation. Seems downright pigheaded, thinks just in tactical terms, with a bit of a tic since Africa about his supply problems."[3]

As it happened, it was Kesselring who read the situation correctly. The location of the landings had been selected by the Allies with air cover in mind. They began on September 3. Montgomery's Eighth Army landed virtually unopposed on the toe of Italy and began to advance rapidly northward. On that very same day the Italians signed an armistice on Sicily, but it was kept secret for the time being. Five days later came the main landings by General Mark Clark's U.S. Fifth Army at Salerno. General Dwight D. Eisenhower, the Supreme Allied Commander in the Mediterranean, broadcast the news of the Italian surrender just before the troops landed, which was an error, since it was not supposed to be transmitted until they were ashore. Before taking action OKW checked with Marshal Badoglio that this was indeed the case and it was not until the evening of the same day, September 8, that Rommel, who was still in Munich, received the code word to put Operation Axis into effect. Communist uprisings in Milan and Turin were speedily put down, and thousands of Italian troops disarmed and sent to prisoner of war camps in Germany. Rommel's subsequent comment was: "What a shameful end for an army!"[4] German troops also speedily occupied Rome and rushed to contain the Salerno beachhead. The one thing that Rommel was unable to do was to prevent the Italian warships in La Spezia escaping out to sea to surrender. On September 9 HQ Army Group B was finally established on Lake Garda and all appeared to be going well. Five days later Rommel was suddenly incapacitated. On the night of September 14 he was stricken by abdominal pains and vomiting. It was appendicitis. He was rushed to hospital and operated on, but was not discharged until September 27. That same afternoon he was summoned to the Wolf's Lair to discuss future strategy in Italy.

While Rommel was in the hospital, Kesselring had launched fierce counterattacks against the Salerno beachhead, but they had failed to eradicate it. The Fifth and Eighth Armies had also linked up. Kesselring had therefore obtained Hitler's permission to make a fighting withdrawal northward, making maximum use of demolitions to impede the Allied advance. Mussolini, too, had been rescued in a daring operation conceived by General Kurt Student, Germany's leading airborne commander, and was now planning to set up a new Fascist republic at Saló in northern Italy. The conference, at which Kesselring was also present, took place on September 30. Both he and Rommel gave situation reports, and Hitler clearly approved of what Kesselring was doing to delay the Allied advance. Indeed, the longer the Allies could be held in southern Italy the better, since it would wear them down. This strategy, of course, ran totally contrary to Rommel's concept of withdrawing to a fortified line in the Apennines north of Rome. Kesselring's position was further strengthened when his proposal to hold the Allies in the mountains south of Rome was accepted by both Hitler and OKW. Rommel pointed out that the plan had an obvious flaw, namely, that the Allies could outflank what became known as the Gustav Line through amphibious landings, which is what they eventually attempted to do at Anzio in January 1944. His objection was ignored.

In spite of Hitler's approving of Kesselring's concept of operations rather than that of Rommel, he did on October 17 tell Rommel that he was to become commander in chief in

Italy and that Kesselring was to be posted to Norway. There was a proviso, though. Rommel had to hold the line selected by Kesselring south of Rome. Rommel objected strongly and demanded a directive that would give him freedom of action. He also apparently added that he believed Italy could not be held for long; his "defeatist" streak was showing through once more. On his return to Lake Garda two days later, he heard from Jodl that written confirmation of his appointment as commander-in-chief was on its way. That same evening he was telephoned by Jodl and told that his appointment was on hold. A few days later Hitler announced that Kesselring was to have the job after all. He preferred the inherent optimism of Smiling Albert (Kesselring's nickname) to the pessimism exuded by Rommel. In a letter to Lucie Rommel wrote: "Maybe I aroused no great hopes that the position would be held, maybe my delay in taking over command was the cause. There may again, of course, be entirely different reasons."[5]

Rommel bade farewell to Italy on November 21, 1943, the day Kesselring formally became Commander-in-Chief Italy, and took the forces controlled by Army Group B under his command. Rommel had been given a new task by Hitler and in Western Europe. The trigger for this fresh assignment was an estimate of the situation written by Gerd von Rundstedt, the Commander-in-Chief West, at the end of October. Up until that time this theater, not being an area of active operations, had been kept relatively starved of troops, especially mobile formations. Much of what Rundstedt had was either low-grade infantry divisions or others that were refitting after fighting on the Eastern Front, none of which stayed with him for long. By autumn 1943 it was clear to him that the Allies would invade Western Europe, and Germany urgently needed to strengthen its forces there. As he pointed out in his estimate, with 1,600 miles of coastline to defend, it was impossible to create a continuous barrier, and he could only cover the coasts through observation posts, rather than physically defend them. While he accepted that the Atlantic Wall, which represented the coastal defenses that had been constructed, did help to deter the Allies—and not least as a propaganda weapon—the battle could only be won with mobile reserves. Yet all he had in theater were three SS panzer grenadier divisions, one of which was only just beginning to form. Hitler took immediate note of this cri de coeur and on November 3 issued Directive No. 51, in which he stated that the defenses in the West were to be immediately strengthened, especially in terms of mobility, antitank capability, and artillery.

It was in this context that Rommel saw Hitler two days after the issue of the directive. Hitler wanted him to carry out a study of the defenses and come up with recommendations to improve them. Rommel was also to retain his HQ Army Group B, which gave Rommel hope that he might be given another operational command. When he heard that Rommel was coming, Rundstedt, who, as he admitted himself, was past his prime and whose health was questionable, actually hoped that Rommel was going to replace him, but a visit from Keitel clarified matters. Keitel told him that there was no intention of Rommel succeeding him, since he was only suitable for "Seydlitz type attacks as at Rossbach, but not for larger strategic operations."[6] (Keitel was alluding to Frederick the Great of Prussia's cavalry commander, Friedrich Seydlitz, who charged the flank of a vastly superior Austro-French army at Rossbach in November 1757 and gained Frederick a stunning victory). As for Rommel, he was delighted with the prospect and was clearly fired up by Hitler: "What power he radiates! And what faith and confidence he inspires in his people!" he noted in his diary on his way back to Italy.[7]

Before starting out on his tour of inspection Rommel was able to snatch a few days with Lucie and Manfred, who were now temporarily living in a villa near Ulm, in Rommel's native Swabia. On December 1, his staff assembled, Rommel boarded a train at Munich and headed for Denmark, where he was to begin his inspection. An invasion of that country was considered unlikely, but Rommel's brief was to inspect the whole of the Atlantic Wall. He noted that, as far as this section of the Atlantic Wall was concerned, there were just a few coastal batteries and that the defense forces were too far inland. Flying back to his headquarters in Munich with his chief engineer, Wilhelm Meise, two weeks later, Rommel began to formulate his ideas. He reasoned that the overwhelming air superiority that the Allies were likely to enjoy would make it very difficult to bring forward supplies. This meant that the Germans would not be able to fight any maneuver battles. Therefore the invasion had to be defeated on the beaches, and so strengthening the coastal defenses was paramount, including deploying the maximum forces close to the coast. Thinking back perhaps to El Alamein, Rommel told Meise that he wanted the beaches and the waters off them strewn with mines.

By the time Rommel returned to Germany a new house had been obtained for his family by the Ulm city authorities. It was in Herrlingen on the outskirts of Ulm and had been a Jewish old people's home until it was confiscated in 1942. Work needed to be done on it before the Rommels could move in, but Rommel was able to inspect it before setting off again, this time for France.

Rommel arrived in France on December 18 and was quartered in a château at Fontainebleau on the outskirts of the French capital. The next day he went to report to Rundstedt, who was living in the prestigious Georges Cinq Hotel in Paris itself. Rundstedt painted Rommel a very gloomy picture of how things stood. The two men were then joined by a number of senior staff officers. General Bodo Zimmermann, Rundstedt's chief of operations, was present and recalled that neither Rommel nor Rundstedt made any attempt at conversation and that "it was a strange, silent meal which will never be forgotten by any man who was present."[8]

The truth was that they were very different characters. Rundstedt was the doyen of the Prussian officer corps and a man who believed in maximum delegation to his staff and abhorred self-advertisement. He also considered, as did many others, that Rommel had won his laurels in a mere sideshow and had no experience of real war as it was being fought on the Eastern Front. He admired Rommel's courage and recognized his ability for low-level operations, but he could not be considered a higher commander, even though Rundstedt was prepared to accept being replaced by him. He also disapproved of Rommel's close contact with Hitler, especially the fact that he would pick up the telephone and speak directly to the Führer, something that Rundstedt would never do.

On his part, Rommel had always had a general dislike of Prussians. He considered Rundstedt to be well past his prime and was horrified at the apparent lethargy of Rundstedt's headquarters and its opulent lifestyle. The two men had to work together, though, especially since the Nazi propaganda machine was making much of Rommel's arrival in the West; Rundstedt was being portrayed as the "guarantee for the security of Fortress Europe against all attempts by the Americans and British to infiltrate, while Rommel was the man of action or led from the front."[9]

Rommel set off once more on his inspection tour. He was personally convinced that the Allied invasion would come on either the Belgian coast or the northern French coast down to and including the River Somme. He therefore made his next visit to General Hans von Salmuth's Fifteenth Army, which was responsible for this sector. He impressed on Salmuth the need to have his forces well forward so that they could launch immediate counterattacks to drive the enemy back into the sea and emphasized the need to sow extensive minefields. He also told the Fifteenth Army commander of a promise that a thousand more fighter aircraft were to be deployed to the West. He then returned to Fontainebleau to write up his findings.

Christmas Day he spent with his staff and the soldiers at his headquarters. He did telephone Lucie and heard that Manfred, now age fifteen, was to be mobilized as a Luftwaffe auxiliary working with antiaircraft guns. Rommel therefore wrote him a letter of advice: "You'll have to learn to obey the orders of your superiors without answering back. Often there'll be orders that don't suit you, or that you don't get the point of. Obey without question. A superior can't go into a long palaver with his subordinates. There just isn't the time to give reasons for every order."[10]

Then it was back to briefing Rundstedt. This time their meeting went much better. Rundstedt approved of Rommel's forward defense strategy and agreed that the most likely point of attack was on either side of the Somme, although Rundstedt also thought that the Pas de Calais, where the English Channel was at its narrowest, was a likely option. The only point of difference was that Rommel wanted the mobile divisions to be close to the coast whereas Rundstedt wanted them concentrated farther back so that they could react in any direction. For the time being, this matter was left unresolved.

Rundstedt was still not clear, however, as to Rommel's position in the chain of command. He sought clarification from OKW and was told that Rommel was under his command except in the event of an invasion of Denmark or the need to occupy Hungary, in which case Rommel's headquarters would be detached from him. In mid-January 1944 the situation was finally resolved when Hitler ruled that Rommel should have operational command of the coastal area stretching from the Netherlands in the north round to the River Loire in France. He would have under him Salmuth's Fifteenth Army and Friedrich Dollmann's Seventh Army, which was covering Normandy and Brittany.

With the coming of the new year Rommel was in a frenzy of activity. He was constantly on the move. He exhorted Salmuth's men to greater efforts to prepare the beach defenses. Salmuth himself felt that his men were having to work too hard and that there was no time for them to carry out other training. He complained to Rommel, saying that his program was overly ambitious. The two had a furious row, but the dust then settled.

It was not until January 22 that Dollmann got a visit from Rommel. Dollmann tried to convince him of the likelihood of Normandy being the Allied landing area and pointed out how stretched his troops were to defend their section of coastline. Rommel, unconvinced, argued that the landings would take place in Salmuth's sector because that presented the shortest route to Germany's main industrial region, the Ruhr. Even so, he thought that Dollmann's troops had been living too soft a life. One of Dollmann's corps commanders who was pleased to see Rommel was Erich Marcks, who had lost a leg in Russia and most of his family in an RAF bombing raid. He wrote to his surviving son: "He's [Rommel] very frank and earnest. He's not just a flash-in-the-pan; he's a real warlord. It's a good thing that AH [Adolf Hitler] thinks a lot of him, for all his bluntness, and gives him these important jobs."[11]

Steadily the defenses of the Atlantic Wall were improved, with numerous obstacles being placed, as well as mines, on the beaches, but it still needed Rommel's ruthless drive to keep everything moving. "Time and again one comes up against bureaucratic and ossified individuals who resist everything new and progressive. But we'll manage it all the same," he wrote to Lucie near the end of January.[12] He covered enormous distances. During the period February 7–11 he drove 1,400 miles to inspect the Atlantic and Mediterranean coastlines of Army Group G, which was responsible for southern France. The defense of these regions was not his responsibility, and the trip a ruse to make the Allies, and indeed the German people, believe that he was everywhere. There is no doubt that Rommel's determination to get things done, whatever obstacles there might be in the way, had a dramatic effect. But there were two unresolved issues.

The first was the debate over where the invasion would come. Rommel was still determined that it would be in Fifteenth Army's sector, but Hitler was beginning to think the same way as Dollmann, that it could come in Normandy or Brittany. The Allies did not help matters. Under the blanket code name of Bodyguard they developed an elaborate series of deception plans designed to tie down German forces elsewhere and divert attention from Normandy. Two of the measures were the establishment of a fictitious British army in Scotland so as to pose a threat to Norway, where sizable German forces were stationed, and another fictional army in southeast England. This unit was commanded by George S. Patton, whom the Allies knew was considered by the Germans the boldest of the Allied generals; his assignment was to make the Germans believe that Pas de Calais was where the landings would take place. Although on a smaller scale, the deception plans prior to Desert Storm in 1991 had many similarities with Bodyguard. To disguise the fact that his main attack would come west of Kuwait, General Schwarzkopf made the Iraqis believe that the main effort would be directly across the Saudi-Kuwait border and would be combined with an amphibious landing by the 4th and 5th U.S. Marine Brigades, which were afloat in the Persian Gulf and carried out some much publicized landing rehearsals.

The other issue also had a connection with the location of the landings. This was the thorny question of the deployment of the armor. Thanks to Directive No. 51 Rundstedt had been receiving the reinforcements he requested, and by March 1944 he had eight panzer and two panzer grenadier divisions in-the-ater. Hitler had also appointed Geyr von Schweppenburg, who had considerable experience of armored warfare on the Eastern Front, to command Panzer Group West, which was under Rundstedt's direct control. Schweppenburg was insistent that the armor be concentrated in the Paris area so that it could re-spond to landings wherever they might come. Rommel con-tinued to demand that it deploy close to the coast, which meant dispersing it. He kept reiterating that most of the com-manders in France had little realization of the might of fire-power that the Western Allies could produce, on land, at sea, and in the air, and that this would make it nigh impossible for the armor to deploy if it was held back. The two had heated discussions on this issue, with neither conceding. In the end Rundstedt stepped in and attempted a compromise, allocating some of the divisions to Rommel, while Schweppenburg re-tained the rest. It satisfied neither man, and there is evidence that Rundstedt was also not happy about the way Rommel was dispersing his armor. Günther Blumentritt, Rundstedt's chief of staff, recalled a discussion that the two men had over the de-ployment of the 2nd Panzer Division. It had been given to Rommel, and he intended to put half of it on one side of the Somme and the rest on the other side of the river. Rundstedt said that he would concentrate the complete division in the

Amiens area, "but as far as I'm concerned, do your own blasted business in your way." Blumentritt also said that Rundstedt would refer to Rommel as Field Marshal Cub, "because he always came in like an unlicked cub."[13] In the end, however, it was Hitler who stepped in and ruled that Army Groups B and G could have three divisions each, while Schweppenburg would retain the remaining four as a reserve. But the Panzer Group West divisions would not be allowed to move without Hitler's permission, a ruling that would cause major problems on D-Day.

In spite of the argument over the armor, Rommel was becoming more confident as the weeks went by and the coast defenses grew stronger. At the end of March he wrote to Lucie: "I saw plenty to cheer me here yesterday. Although we've still a lot of weaknesses, we're looking forward full of confidence to what's coming."[14] He had by now moved to a new headquarters closer to the coast, a picturesque château at La Roche-Guyon, a small village on the River Seine between Mantes and Vernon. It was the seat of the Duke de La Rochefoucauld, who continued to live there with his family and for whom Rommel formed an instant liking. He also had a new chief of staff, Hans Speidel. In March 1944 Rommel had gone on ten days' leave to Herrlingen and invited Gause and his wife to stay. Apparently, Lucie did get not along with Frau Gause and demanded of Erwin that he replace his chief of staff. Rommel appears to have meekly complied with his wife's wishes and from the two possibilities offered to him by OKH chose Speidel, a fellow Swabian, whom he had first met in 1915 and known between the wars. Speidel was academic and polished in manner and enjoyed the arts. He was thus the perfect foil to Rommel, who wrote to Lucie shortly after he arrived: "He makes a good fresh impression. I think I'm going to get on well with him." What Rommel did not know was that Speidel was one of those who were plotting to remove Hitler. One thing that Speidel did quickly succeed in doing was to get Rommel to relax more, which in itself was no mean achievement given Rommel's constant restlessness. He encouraged Rommel to go for walks with two terriers he had acquired and to hunt game, a pursuit Rommel had always enjoyed, with the local French landowners.

By the beginning of May it was widely expected the Allies would invade that month. Hitler was still convinced that Normandy was the objective and sent additional troops to Dollmann, including the 91st Air Landing Division, which had been specially trained to deal with enemy paratroops. Rommel visited Normandy again, but noticed that the Allies' air activity was considerably less there than it was in Salmuth's sector, which reinforced his own view that it was Fifteenth Army that would face the invasion. In fact, the Allied air forces had launched a campaign to cut the road and rail routes leading into Normandy and to destroy as much as possible of the Luftwaffe in the West. To disguise the former, they attacked targets throughout northern and central France and Belgium. Yet as the month wore on and the Allies made no move, the tension eased. Some wondered whether the Allies were going to come at all; the activity might be a bluff to disguise impending operations elsewhere. On May 30 Rundstedt informed OKW that there was no immediate danger of invasion. A forecast of worsening weather over the next few days also reinforced the belief that no invasion was imminent. He agreed that Rommel could go back to Germany on June 5, both to enjoy a few more days' leave and to see Hitler so as to ask him for more reinforcements. The commander in chief had apparently finally grown to like Rommel, largely as a result of an informal lunch they had together on May 27, which enabled them to better know one another. Dollmann organized a map exercise for his senior officers for June 5 at Rennes. Rundstedt himself planned to go off on a tour of inspection starting on June 6.

The first indications that the invasion actually was under way came with a BBC coded broadcast to the French Resistance on the evening of June 5. Rundstedt ordered a heightened state of alertness and warned of the likelihood of increased sabotage activity. Then came reports of paratroops dropping at the base of the Cotentin Peninsula and to the east of Caen. Normandy was clearly under attack. Rundstedt now telephoned OKW to demand that the panzer reserves be placed under his command. He was told that Hitler was asleep and could not be disturbed. He then had a signal sent, but there was no immediate response to it. By now dawn was breaking and the coastal batteries were being bombed from the air. After this they were engaged by naval guns, and landing craft began to make for the shore. The defenders were experiencing something of the "shock and awe" that immediately preceded the 2003 invasion of Iraq. The one mobile division in the area was the reconstituted 21st Panzer. Its commander had been in Paris and did not get back to his headquarters until 6:00 A.M. It was first sent to deal with the British airborne landing east of Caen, but then, when British troops began to land on the beaches north of the city, was ordered to deal with them. Because its units were initially scattered, it took time to organize them, and the switch of mission added to the confusion. It was therefore not until the late afternoon that the attack got going. One battle group did succeed in reaching the coast between the British beachhead and that of the neighboring Canadians but turned back when it saw aircraft dropping parachutes for fear of being cut off. That was the sum of the D-Day counterattacks that Rommel believed would drive the Allies back into the sea. As for the panzer reserves, Keitel, having spoken to Hitler, telephoned Rundstedt at 10:00 A.M. to say that his request to transfer them to his command had been rejected. He could, however move the 12th SS Panzer Grenadier Division, made up of fanatical former Hitler Youth members, nearer the coast and that the Panzer Lehr, a crack division commanded by Rommel's old comrade in arms Fritz Bayerlein, would be placed on standby to move. In the afternoon came a further relaxation. OKW said that Rundstedt could now have the 17th SS Panzer Grenadier Division and the Leibstandarte, which with the Hitler Youth Division made up Sepp Dietrich's I SS Panzer Corps. The Liebstandarte, however, was still refitting in Belgium and would not be available for some time. Therefore, Rundstedt placed the Panzer Lehr and 21st Panzer Division under Dietrich's command in order to mount a counterattack on June 7 and sent the 17th Panzer Grenadier Division to confront the Americans in the west. By nightfall on June 6, the Allies had some 155,000 men ashore in five beachheads on a thirty-mile front. The Germans had been largely caught by surprise, and they still were not certain that these were the main landings, since Allied deception measures were continuing to point toward the Pas de Calais.

But what of Rommel? He had gone straight to Herrlingen, for Lucie's fiftieth birthday, which was on June 6. Among the presents that he was keen to give his wife was a pair of shoes that he had had specially made for her in Paris. He now received a telephone call from Speidel saying that the invasion had begun. It brought an abrupt end to the birthday celebration. Rommel set off immediately for France. He arrived back at La Roche-Guyon at 10:00 P.M. that night. His artillery commander, Hans Lottmann, noted in his diary: "He's very calm and collected. Grim-faced, as to be expected."[15] Briefed on the situation, Rommel concurred with the plan for Dietrich to mount a counterattack in the morning. The attack, however, did not take place then since it took the Hitler Youth Division time to arrive, thanks to Allied air activity.

A blow-by-blow account of the Battle of Normandy would be out of place here. Suffice it to say that the Allies soon linked up their beachheads and began to advance inland. The Germans fought desperately, and the Allied advance was slow, but at a pace sufficient to keep the defenders very stretched. The move of the reserve mobile divisions to the front was bedeviled by the destruction of road and rail bridges, both as a result of Allied bombing and the activities of the French Resistance. The result was that these divisions found themselves holding the line rather than being held back to mount a major counterattack. Matters were not helped by the fact that Rundstedt and Rommel believed for some time that there was still to be a landing in the Pas de Calais. For this reason neither the two panzer divisions allocated to the Fifteenth Army nor any other formations under Salmuth's command were deployed to Normandy for some days. Rommel, as usual, was tireless in visiting the front, even down to divisional headquarters level to encourage and imbue a determination to resist. Orders from Hitler to mount major counterattacks were simply impossible to carry out given the intense pressure that Rommel's troops were under, as were demands that not an inch of ground be given. It had echoes of El Alamein. Rundstedt and Rommel became so frustrated that they asked that Hitler come and see for himself.

Hitler eventually agreed to met the two field marshals at Margival, near Soissons, on June 17. The meeting took place in a railway tunnel on top of which there was a collection of bunkers built as Hitler's field headquarters for the great nonevent of 1940, the invasion of Britain. All but Hitler stood, while he sat on a stool. At the time the Americans were threatening to seal off the base of the Cotentin Peninsula prior to advancing north to seize Cherbourg, which they intended should become the Allies' main supply port. Hitler had, however, declared that Cherbourg must be held.

Rundstedt made a few remarks and then handed the floor to Rommel. Rommel said that it was merely a waste of troops to try to hold Cherbourg. The Allied pressure elsewhere meant that the only answer was a limited withdrawal so that the German forces would be out of range of the Allies' naval gunfire, which was proving particularly devastating. Rommel then declared that he planned on placing the panzer divisions on the flanks to mount a double enveloping counterattack. He also reiterated that reinforcements had to be sent to Normandy if the battle was not to be irretrievably lost. He demanded freedom of action to fight the battle as he and Rundstedt wanted.

Hitler took little notice of his generals' remarks and launched into one of his customary long monologues. Hitler declared that the V-weapon offensive just launched against Britain would bring that country to its knees. An air raid warning then sounded and the party moved to more protective shelter. It was either then or when Hitler was walking to his car at the end of the conference that the two field marshals raised the question of putting out peace feelers to the Western Allies. Hitler's response was that "fanatical resistance" was the only course open, especially in light of the Allies' demand for unconditional surrender.[16]

Rundstedt came away from the conference sunk in gloom. In contrast, Rommel's spirits appear to have been uplifted. He wrote to Lucie on the following day: "A quick breakthrough to Paris is now hardly a possibility. We've got a lot of good stuff coming up. The Führer was very cordial and in a very good humor. He realizes the gravity of the situation."[17] There were three reasons for this. Once more he had been mesmerized by Hitler's delivery. He had also been told by Jodl, who was present, that further reinforcements were on the way, including two SS panzer divisions, and Hitler had agreed to visit Rommel at La Roche-Guyon the next day. That did not happen. A defective V–1 flying bomb hit Margival that very same evening, and Hitler and his entourage immediately left for Germany without a word to Rundstedt or Rommel.

Hitler continued to insist that Cherbourg be held and that there would be no withdrawals. Rommel's disillusion soon set in again, doubtless encouraged by Speidel. Cherbourg fell on June 27, and the pressure continued unabated on the main Normandy Front. On the previous day Rundstedt and Rommel had once more demanded to be allowed freedom of action. The response from OKW was to summon them both to Berchtesgaden for a conference with Hitler on June 29. They were not allowed to fly or go by train. Hence they had to make the six-hundred-mile journey by car. Once more Hitler launched into a monologue about the miracle weapons that would change the course of the war. As for Normandy, they must halt the Allies and then eradicate their beachhead. To make matters worse, the Russians had launched a major offensive, and Rundstedt and Rommel knew that they were unlikely to receive much more in the way of reinforcements. The situation seemed impossible. And their gloom deepened. Hitler had also just demanded an investigation into why Cherbourg had fallen, making it clear that he wanted Dollmann's head, since the port was a Seventh Army responsibility. As it happened, Rundstedt and Rommel had just heard that he had died of a heart attack. They therefore demanded that the investigation be dropped. They also once more raised the possibility of peace feelers being put out to the Allies. Again Hitler dismissed this suggestion out of hand.

Rundstedt and Rommel arrived back at their respective headquarters late on June 30 to be met by further demands for a counterattack, this time against the British, who had just made some ground in an operation code-named Epsom. Their subordinate commanders were clamoring for a withdrawal; Schweppenburg especially wanted to give his hard-pressed panzer divisions a breathing space so that they would be capable of future offensive operations. Rundstedt raised the matter with OKW and received the reply that in no circumstances were there to be any withdrawals. By now totally exasperated, Rundstedt told Keitel on the telephone that he could not carry on any longer under these conditions. The next morning, July 2, Rundstedt attended Dollmann's funeral in Paris with Rommel. After this Rundstedt was told that he was being relieved by Günther von Kluge, but was being awarded the Oak Leaves to his Knight's Cross as a farewell present from Hitler.

Rommel may have hoped that he would take over from Rundstedt, but he now had to accept the new incumbent, who had spent the last few days in Hitler's company being primed for the job, an indication that Hitler had already decided to sack Rundstedt before his outburst to Keitel. Kluge visited him at his headquarters on the following day and made plain to him that there would be no withdrawals and that Rommel was not to go behind his back and speak to Hitler directly. Not surprisingly, Rommel took an instant dislike to his new boss. Speidel continued to work on Rommel to put out peace feelers himself and had established a means of communication with the Allies via the International Red Cross. Rommel was also visited by another of the plotters, Luftwaffe Colonel Cäsar von Hofacker, although no evidence of their conversation survives. Apparently, though, he was not prepared to act on his own and felt that the support of other senior commanders in the West was vital, of whom Kluge was clearly not prepared to give. Rommel also had a desperate battle on his hands, that for Caen. The British were determined to take it, but were being frustrated by the dogged defense put up by the Hitler Youth Division. This battle and the continuing American pressure in the west kept him fully occupied for the next ten days. Then came indications that the British were about to mount a major attack to finally engulf Caen. On July 17 Rommel drove up to see Dietrich to ensure that he was ready to receive the attack. Helmuth Lang, Rommel's aide, recorded that Rommel asked Dietrich if he would obey Rommel's orders even if they contradicted Hitler's, to which Sepp Dietrich, who had a great admiration for Rommel, replied in the affirmative. Once back in the car, Rommel told Lange: "I've won Dietrich over."[18] Shortly afterward, a marauding Allied fighter-bomber spotted the car and attacked it. Both the driver and Rommel were hit, the former fatally, and the car careered off the road, hit a tree, and rebounded into a ditch, throwing the occupants out. Rommel's skull was fractured. He was evacuated to a Luftwaffe hospital thirty miles away.

Three days later, far off at the Wolf's Lair, there was a bomb explosion in the middle of one of Hitler's conferences. In Paris the German governor, General Heinrich von Stülpnagel, who was in on the plot, immediately arrested all the SS elements in the city and then looked for support to Kluge, who had quickly become disillusioned by what was happening in Normandy. In Berlin, the plot was centered on the headquarters of the Home Army, which was responsible for training and reserves. Its staff waited for confirmation that Hitler was dead. Colonel Klaus von Stauffenberg, who had placed the bomb under the conference table, arrived there certain that Hitler had been killed. Goebbels, who was in Berlin, heard that Hitler was still alive and ordered the Berlin Guard Battalion, which was commanded by a dedicated Nazi, to arrest the plotters. Some, including Stauffenberg, were summarily shot. In Paris, Stülpnagel received no support from Kluge, who had also heard that Hitler had survived. He was therefore forced to release his prisoners, and his fate was sealed. Hitler's secret police, the Gestapo, launched a wide-ranging investigation and soon identified a number of senior officers. They could not, however, be tried by a civilian court, and so a Court of Honor was established to strip them of their rank. They were then arraigned before a court in Berlin, found guilty, and hanged from meat hooks in Ploetzensee Prison. After the first few sessions of the Court of Honor and as the Gestapo net spread ever wider Rundstedt was brought in by Hitler to preside over the court, so as to give the proceedings some respectability.

All this passed Rommel by. He was moved to a hospital in Paris, delirious for much of the time. Then, on August 8, much improved in health, he was taken back to Herrlingen. He was saddened by the arrest of so many friends and acquaintances. He also heard that Kluge had been sacked in mid-August and summoned back to Berlin, but had committed suicide en route. Yet Rommel was opposed to the assassination of Hitler because he believed that it would merely add civil war to Germany's woes. Rather, he thought that surrender in the field was the only option, but this needed the overall support of the fighting troops, which would be difficult to procure when they were locked in mortal combat.

By then the Battle of Normandy had been lost, and the remnants of Army Group B would soon begin retreating from northern France. Indeed, the news became more depressing by the day. In September came word that Speidel had been dismissed from his post, and Rommel began to sense that the net was closing round him as well. This felt even more so when Speidel was arrested.

On October 7 Keitel asked Rommel to report to Berlin; a special train would be provided to take him there. When Rommel asked the reason, he was told it was to discuss his future employment. He declined on health grounds. Six days later he received a message that two representatives from OKW would call on him at home.

On October 14 Manfred Rommel arrived home, having been given a brief leave from his antiaircraft battery. His father told him that he was expecting two generals who would come to discuss his future. They duly arrived at midday, and Rommel was alone with them for forty-five minutes. They told him that they had been sent by Keitel on Hitler's orders. Evidence from Stülpnagel, Speidel, Hofacker, and others had implicated him in the plot on Hitler's life. Because of his high standing with the German people, Hitler was giving him two options. Either he could be arraigned before a People's Court, in which case Lucie and Manfred were likely to suffer as well, or he could take his own life and be given a state funeral and his family would not be harmed. Rommel immediately chose the second option. He then explained this to Lucie and Manfred, stating that he was quite prepared to declare and prove his innocence in court, but he would not allow them to suffer the consequences. Generals Wilhelm Burgdorf and Ernst Maisel gave him a cyanide tablet and then took him out to the car. Fifteen minutes later they arrived at a local hospital with Rommel's corpse. He had died of a heart attack, they said.

CHAPTER 7

Rommel's Legacy

ERWIN ROMMEL DULY HAD HIS STATE FUNERAL. IT WAS organized with meticulous precision by the Nazi hierarchy for October 18 at the Rathaus in Ulm. A special train was arranged to leave Berlin the previous evening with distinguished mourners on board. Field Marshal Gerd von Rundstedt, who had been restored as Commander-in-Chief West, was nominated as Hitler's personal representative and was scheduled to arrive at the town hall at 1:00 P.M. Two companies of soldiers and a mixed company of naval, air, and Waffen SS, together with a military band, provided the escort.

The ceremony opened with a rendering of the second movement of Beethoven's Third Symphony, the *Eroica,* and then Rundstedt addressed the vast assembly. He spoke of

Rommel's military talents, especially in relation to his achievements in France and North Africa. Rommel was a true National Socialist whose "heart belonged to the Führer." Then, addressing the bier, Rundstedt declared: "Your heroism shows us all, again, the watchword 'Fight until victory.'"[1] Admiral Friedrich Ruge, who had been on Rommel's staff in Normandy, was present and commented that "although curiously impersonal and somewhat restrained, it was a good speech to those who did not know what was being played out."[2] Rundstedt then laid Hitler's wreath at the bier and took his place beside Rommel's widow. The coffin was now taken to the crematorium and the ashes then interred in the Herrlingen cemetery.

Lengthy obituaries appeared in the Nazi press. Even *The Times* of London carried one. While giving muted praise to Rommel's tactical ability, the *Times* was otherwise very inaccurate, claiming among other things that he had been a member of the Nazi Party since its beginning. Hitler, too, published a special order of the day, and later, in March 1945, when the war was all but over, informed Lucie that he had commissioned a statue of her husband. Needless to say, it came to nothing.

The true details of Rommel's death came out at the end of the war, and then he became inextricably linked to the July 1944 bomb plot even though he had not been connected to it. He came to be regarded as a "good German" by both sides of World War II. Thus, when the eminent military theorist Basil Liddell Hart published *The Rommel Papers,* a collection of Rommel's World War II writings and letters, in 1953, it became an instant bestseller. When the new German Federal Republic re-established the German armed forces in the 1950s under the name Bundeswehr, the authorities were careful to create them afresh and to sever any connection with Hitler's

Wehrmacht. There was, however, a barracks at Augustdorf, near Detmold, that was named for Rommel, an honor not given to any other of Hitler's field marshals. There was, too, a tendency to airbrush the close connections that Rommel had had with Hitler for much of the war.

What, though, is relevant today in the life of Rommel? While he cannot be considered a master strategist, he does stand as one of history's great fighting generals because he was imbued with many of the qualities that soldiers hold dear. In courage and leadership there are few who can match him. He came close to death many times, especially during World War I, in France in 1940, and in North Africa. Some might say that he led a charmed life, and certainly the doctors who treated him after his wounding in July 1944 were amazed that he survived the quadruple skull fracture that he suffered. When it came to leadership, there is no doubt but that Rommel possessed extraordinary charisma. Some of this can be attributed to his personal bravery, which he demonstrated so often. He led from the front. Time and again we have seen him dashing to the critical point on the battlefield and leading his troops forward. Rommel was also a great believer in not expecting his men to undertake anything that he was not prepared to do himself. In this respect he attached great importance to his own physical fitness. He did not smoke. He drank alcohol but seldom and then in extreme moderation. Indeed, his lifestyle was spartan, at least in the field. He was perfectly content to eat the same rations as his men and had little interest in luxuries. This made his men feel that he was one of them. He was also prepared to get his hands dirty—helping to dig out a bogged vehicle or marshaling traffic are but two examples. He felt it important to be seen by his men. He was constantly on the move visiting units and seeing for himself that his orders were being carried out. Indeed, he is very like the modern chief executive officer who does not confine himself to his corporate office or conference room, but is prepared to get out on the shop floor to obtain a true feel for the pulse of his business. Rommel was also a blunt speaker, who said what he thought. He had a temper, but his explosions of fury never lasted long.

Rommel drove himself and his men hard at times, to his own detriment. At no time did this become more apparent than in summer 1942. The strain that Rommel put on himself meant that his health did break down. Accompanying the physical manifestations that he suffered came an uncharacteristic bout of indecision. He had denied himself sleep and pushed his body too hard. This was in contrast to the equally ascetic Bernard Montgomery, who insisted on having a good night's sleep, which was not to be disturbed under any circumstances: only in this way, he believed, could he keep himself fresh. The contrast illustrates well the point that a commander must take care of himself.

This leads to the question of Rommel's style of command. The first point to note is that Rommel was a great believer in the value of reconnaissance. Whenever possible, he examined the terrain over which he was about to fight. It was one of the keys to his success in France, Romania, and Italy during 1914–1918. When time or the situation did not permit a survey, a careful map study was a very good substitute. From 1940 his reconnaissance was often done from the air, using his Storch light aircraft. In line with German practice of the time he liked to keep his written orders as short as possible, and they were mission oriented, which means that the commander's aim is clearly defined for his subordinates, and they are given the maximum possible latitude in the methods they use to achieve it. The Germans call it *Auftragstaktik*. It worked particularly well for them, especially during the early World War II blitzkrieg campaigns. Not, however, for another thirty years or more would the North Atlantic Treaty Organization begin to adopt this concept; it certainly proved its worth in the two wars against Iraq. By the same token, Rommel liked to operate with minimum control from above; he became very frustrated when he was not allowed freedom of action. This constraint was especially felt in Italy in 1943 and Normandy in 1944. On the other hand, it should be pointed out that commanders nowadays find themselves often having to operate on very much tighter political restrictions than existed in World War II. This usually means strict rules of engagement, which inevitably means closer supervision of subordinates to ensure that they are being observed. This was particularly so in the Balkans in the 1990s and is very much in evidence in Afghanistan, where collateral damage in the shape of killing and wounding innocent civilians turns hearts and minds against NATO and in the tribal territories of Pakistan reduces cooperation from that government.

Rommel also had *Fingerspitzengefühl,* or "subtle intuition," when it came to the battlefield. His ability to sense the critical sector, especially when it came to his opponent's weaknesses, was not something that he was taught but an instinct with which he was lucky enough to be imbued. With this came his ability to quickly take advantage of any opening and exploit it. It was to a significant extent the reason why he preferred to operate with a very small mobile command post—his own vehicle, a signals truck, and possibly a small escort—leaving at his main headquarters a chief of staff empowered to make decisions in his commander's absence and answer for him to ,higher command. This worked particularly well in France in 1940 with the 7th Panzer Division and in the early desert campaigns, when he was able to personally spur his troops to move rapidly to gain the victory that he sensed was within his grasp. Indeed, the operations of the Ghost Division resemble those of General Barry McCaffrey's 24th Infantry Division (Mechanized) in the 1991 Gulf War. It advanced 230 miles in just 100 hours and severed the Iraqi lines of communication between Kuwait and Iraq. The only major exception to this pattern of Rommel's operations was during Operation Crusader, the November 1941 British counteroffensive in Libya, when Rommel made the mistake of taking his chief of staff with him when he made his "dash for the Wire." The larger the span of his command grew, however, the more he found himself having to remain at his main headquarters and had to content himself with merely visiting subordinate headquarters.

Pace of operations was crucial to Rommel's success. If he had been still alive, he would have certainly supported the concept evolved in the 1980s by former fighter pilot Colonel John Boyd of the U.S. Air Force. His conclusion from a study of fighter tactics was that the pilot who summed up the situation, decided on a plan, and put it into action faster than his opponent would be bound to shoot him down. Rommel's Boyd Cycle (also known as OODA: Observation, Orientation, Decision, Action) was consistently inside that of his enemy in his heyday. Much of this was brought about by his ability to surprise, usually through arriving from an unexpected direction. His exploits with his mountain troops during 1916–1918 are littered with examples of this. Indeed, he developed much of his modus operandi in World War II from what he had learned in World War I. It was just that by 1939 armor was better at putting it into effect than infantry on their feet, as he quickly realized from his observations of the campaign in Poland.

Rommel fully understood the vital importance of logistics in his operations. His dilemma in North Africa was that he often did not have enough resources to support what he wanted to achieve. The problem was that the control of those being sent to him was not his. It was the province of Commando Supremo in Rome, for it was Italian ships that had to carry them across the Mediterranean. It was also the Italians who controlled the entry port of Tripoli, and also those of Benghazi and Tobruk when they were in Axis hands. True, Italian bureaucracy played its part in holding up delivery of supplies to the front, but part of the problem was the nature of the Desert War. It was marked by dramatic advances by each side in turn, resulting in overstretched supply lines and hence making the attacker vulnerable. But there was a further difficulty. While the British supply line that went round the tip of South Africa was relatively secure, although the passage took some time, that across the Mediterranean was not. British aircraft from North Africa and Malta, as well as submarines and the Royal Navy's Mediterranean Fleet, made this supply line vulnerable. This was aggravated by Ultra, which was able to identify Rommel's particular shortages, especially fuel. Thus, it was able to establish when tankers were sailing from Italian ports and invite their destruction. Yet however much Rommel might rant and rave over his shortage of supplies, he never used it as an excuse for inaction. He would always opt for positive action, even though it represented a gamble, rather than sit on his hands. It was in his nature. Today there is perhaps more emphasis in having the logistics in place before mounting an operation, but the risks are still there. Afghanistan, for instance, is a logistician's nightmare. A totally landlocked country, far away from Europe and still farther from the United States, the fuel land routes into it are vulnerable. In the south those from Pakistan are prone to attack by the Taliban, especially in the Khyber Pass, while those in the north are subject to Russian acquiescence to NATO's use of them. The majority of supplies therefore have to be flown in, a highly expensive exercise. The commanders on the ground are not prepared to mount major operations without the logistics to back them up, not least because the West is far more politically sensitive to casualties among its forces than it was sixty-five years ago.

His time in North Africa and Italy during World War II brought Rommel into the realm of coalition warfare. His problem was that he formed a low opinion of his Italian ally from the very outset and was not afraid to let it be known. True, he did in time get to like one or two Italian commanders, notably those in XX Corps, which contained the armor and fought closely with the DAK. His general view was that the Italian soldier, if properly led, could fight as well as anyone. There were two obstacles to improving his effectiveness. First, the Italian army's equipment was generally very poor, both in weapons and transportation. Second, Rommel formed the opinion that the officer corps was generally of poor quality and much too concerned with the comforts of life—shades of many Argentinean officers in the Falklands in 1982. Matters were not helped by the complicated command structure that existed in North Africa. Rommel was nominally under Italian command but was given a degree of latitude that was sometimes ill defined. He was also answerable to Kesselring as the German theater commander and did have a direct line to Hitler, via OKW. It can be argued that Schwarzkopf had an equally difficult situation in the Gulf in 1991. He was personally answerable to Washington, D.C., but he also had to recognize that each national contingent within the coalition had the right of appeal to its own government and that he had to be particularly careful to recognize the sensitivities of the Saudis, who in 1990–91 provided the base of operations for Desert Storm, and the other Arab members of the coalition. Schwarzkopf recognized this and succeeded in binding the coalition through tact and diplomacy. Rommel, on the other hand, was too impatient and too blunt. Indeed, since the twenty-first century is so far dominated by coalition warfare, at least as far as the Western democracies are concerned, soldiers have to be totally aware of the politics involved to be effective. In contrast, Rommel only thought in a military context. And that is the main reason why he probably would not have made a good theater commander.

This conclusion brings us to the subject of Rommel and the Nazi regime. There is no doubt that the bulk of the German officer corps welcomed Hitler once he began to rearm Germany. True, some of the old Prussian Junkers, like Rundstedt, were ambivalent. After all, Hitler had been a mere corporal in World War I and spoke with an Austrian accent. Most of them were reassured after the Night of the Long Knives in June 1934, when Hitler crushed the power of the Sturmabteilung, the SA, and confirmed the army's mission as the true defender of the Reich. So relieved were they that they swore a new oath of loyalty to him personally rather than to the state. This *Vereidigung* (oath-taking) immediately put the officer corps in a corner, since it was traditionally imbued with the principle that the loyalty oath was totally binding; in return it received certain privileges, including that an officer could not be tried before a civil court, whatever the offense. The fact that Hitler got away with what at the time seemed to many officers to be dangerous gambles—the military reoccupation of the Rhineland, the annexation of Austria, and the dismemberment of Czechoslovakia—increased their respect for him. That they were apolitical enabled them to close their minds to the regime's growing excesses, notably those against the Jews. Rommel, who witnessed many of these events at Hitler's side, developed growing admiration for the leader who was making Germany great again. There was widespread support in the Wehrmacht for the invasion of Poland. The

Polish Corridor that physically separated East Prussia from the rest of the Reich was an indignity that could no longer be borne, and if the Poles were not prepared to negotiate a solution, war was the only option. There was concern that France and Britain had now been drawn into the war, but in the summer of 1940 Hitler defeated both in just six weeks. (His predecessors had failed to do the same in more than four years' effort some twenty years before.) If it were not for Britain's intransigence, many thought, the war would have been over then.

Rommel himself had many reasons to be personally grateful to Hitler. After all, Hitler had arranged for Rommel to take command of a panzer division, and that had led to his becoming a household name in Germany. It was Hitler, too, who had sent him to North Africa and greater fame and who continued to take much personal interest in him. For others, though, it was the invasion of Russia that caused doubts to begin to surface. This, they thought, was a gamble too far. Hitler's growing interference in the conduct of the campaign aggravated the doubts, but it was not until the surrender at Stalingrad in February 1943 that serious plotting to remove Hitler began to take place. Rommel, however, was too engrossed in North Africa to take much notice of what was happening on the Eastern Front and still maintained his faith in Hitler. His dislike of those whom Hitler had chosen to surround him grew, however. In particular, he blamed Keitel and Jodl for their obstruction of his demands. This was especially when Hitler came down on Kesselring's side over how the campaign in Italy should be conducted. But even after this snub, Rommel still had faith in the Führer. It was not until the Allies invaded France in June 1944 that this faith evaporated. Even then he was faced with a dilemma. He knew by now that the longer the war went on, the greater would be the suffering of Germany, for Hitler was not prepared to think of peace. Meanwhile, Rommel was fighting a desperate battle to contain the Allies, and fearing that Hitler's removal would result in a power vacuum, since there was no obvious figurehead to put in his place. Rommel did not seem to see any clear answer. The only possibility was a unilateral surrender, but this could not be done without the support of the majority of the fighting men, and there appeared to be no way this could be achieved given that they were locked on battle on all fronts. One might therefore argue that Rommel's wounding in July resolved his personal dilemma, but this was only to be temporary, and events soon caught up with him.

The Rommel dilemma is not a problem that senior commanders in Western democracies have had to face, with but one exception: Charles de Gaulle's decision in 1960 to grant independence to Algeria, which ended a war but brought about a short-lived revolt by elements of the French forces that had been fighting there. It is relatively commonplace in the second and third worlds, though, where the military has often overthrown what it has seen as corrupt civil government and then been reluctant to hand back to the people the reins of power. Whether thoughts of unilateral surrender or of killing Saddam Hussein crossed the minds of his generals as they prepared to face the military might of the coalition in 2003 is still a matter of conjecture.

Rommel was not a strategist, but he was a master of the operational and tactical levels of war. As a junior leader in World War I and as a divisional, corps, and army commander during 1940–42, he provides an object lesson in leadership and tactical flair. Although he had his faults, not least a blindness to the evil of the regime he served, they are outshone by his unique qualities. He will continue to be studied with profit for many years to come.

Afterword

FIELD MARSHAL ERWIN ROMMEL WAS UNDOUBTEDLY one of the most charismatic World War II general officers. Here, Charles Messenger focuses on Rommel the tactician, ultimately showing, correctly, that his tactical skills in conjunction with his personal bravery and courage made him a military leader who is still worth remembering and who should be seen as model for today's officers.

Messenger indicates that Rommel had difficulties at the operational level—which at the time meant mastering the three dimensions of battle: the land, air, and naval forces. Today's flag officers need to be capable of coping with an additional fourth dimension, cyber space. Rommel was not a strategist either. Had he been one he would have asked for a political agreement between Germany and Italy regarding the strategic objective of the African Campaign before the operation was launched. But there was no such agreement, so he had to experience what officers often experience today in allied operations: The less precise the strategic objective, the bigger the impediments in conducting combined and joint operations. Rommel's way out in Africa—bypassing the chain of command by seeking direct access to Hitler—must never be taken as an example to be followed. It is one of the battle-proven principles that unity of command must be preserved. Rommel did not pay heed to this principle. That allowed him occasionally to win tactically, but it was also this very attitude that eventually contributed to the failure at the operational, let alone strategic, level in Africa.

Rommel was used by the Nazi Regime to create a myth. He tolerated this since he had a strong dose of personal ambition and vanity. He was not a Nazi, but he welcomed Hitler's coming to power and he was not opposed to Hitler's wars. He was not part of the German resistance against Hitler.

What is known of Rommel for sure was that he was strictly opposed to any idea of assassinating Hitler and that he was in favor of peace talks with the Western powers. It might well be that it was the latter insistence that led to his suicide: The regime simply could not tolerate that the war hero Rommel saw the war as lost.

Beyond details of Rommel's relationship with the Nazi Regime, there are a number of valid lessons to be drawn from Rommel's legacy:

1. The principle of *Auftragstaktik,* which requires military leaders of all levels of command to be fully aware of their superiors' intentions, to act accordingly, if necessary independently, and to achieve the set objective. Needless to say, this can best be achieved by women and men who are truly free.

2. The lasting obligation of military leaders at all levels is to be brave, to set an example of personal valor and to never demand anything to be done what one is not prepared to do oneself.

3. The unchanged necessity to lead from the front in critical situations, although this must never mean not to dispose of the indispensable C⁴ISR.*

Per the series model, Messenger occasionally links Rommel's actions to the realities of contemporary operations. The nature of war has changed greatly over the years. Contemporary military operations are usually operations other than outright war, although they are treated as war by the tactical leaders. But none of today's conflicts is existential for the nations involved. This might well be the main reason for the tight rules of engagement and the lamentable tendency of some politicians to micro-manage military operations.

Rommel's qualities that are most applicable to the realities of today's operations are, at the tactical level, bravery and the preparedness to lead from the front. With vivid prose, Messenger's book delivers this important lesson to the reader. It therefore must be read by anyone who wants to lead.

—General Klaus Naumann

---

* Command, Control, Communications, Computers, Intelligence, Surveillance, and Reconnaissance.

Notes

Introduction

1. Schmidt, *With Rommel in the Desert,* p. 11.

Chapter 1

1. Rommel, *Infantry Attacks,* p. 52.
2. Ibid., p. 75.
3. Ibid., p. 175.
4. Ibid., p. 265.
5. Irving, *Trail of the Fox,* pp. 20–21.
6. Fraser, *Knight's Cross,* p. 98.
7. Irving, p. 33.
8. Ibid., p. 36.

Chapter 2

1. Irving, *Trail of the Fox,* p. 38.
2. Liddell Hart, ed., *Rommel Papers,* p. 6.
3. Ibid., p. 7.
4. Ibid., p. 17.
5. Messenger, *Last Prussian,* p. 113.
6. Liddell Hart, p. 43.

Chapter 3

1. Irving, *Trail of the Fox*, p. 51.
2. Ibid., p. 57.
3. Liddell Hart, ed., *Rommel Papers*, p. 99.
4. Ibid., p. 110.
5. Ibid., p. 140.
6. Burdick and Jacobsen, *Halder War Diaries*, p. 385.
7. Ibid., p. 454.
8. Liddell Hart, p. 150.
9. Ibid., p. 168.
10. Behrendt, *Rommel's Intelligence in the Desert Campaign*, p. 116.

Chapter 4

1. Liddell Hart, *Rommel Papers*, p. 180.
2. Ibid., p. 181.
3. Ibid., p. 183.
4. Irving, *Trail of the Fox*, p. 148.
5. Ibid., p.151.
6. Fraser, *Knight's Cross*, p. 309.
7. Warner, *Auchinleck,* p. 239n.
8. Liddell Hart, p. 204.
9. Ibid., p. 209.
10. Ibid., p. 212.
11. Fraser, p. 337.
12. Liddell Hart, p. 232.
13. Ibid., p. 239.
14. Ibid., p. 248.
15. Messenger, *Unknown Alamein*, p. 52.
16. HQ Panzer Army Africa War Diary, Appendices. Copy in author's possession.
17. Liddell Hart, p. 263.
18. HQ Panzer Army Africa War Diary, op. cit.
19. Liddell Hart, p. 271n.
20. Ibid., p. 271.
21. HQ Panzer Army, Africa War Diary, op. cit.

Chapter 5

1. Liddell Hart, *Rommel Papers*, p. 275, 275n.

2. Irving, *Trail of the Fox*, p. 194.
3. Ibid., pp. 197–98.
4. Ibid.
5. Liddell Hart, p. 302.
6. Ibid., p. 304.
7. Ibid., p. 310.
8. Ibid., p. 314.
9. Irving, p. 209.
10. Ibid., p. 210.
11. Ibid., p. 211.
12. Liddell Hart, p. 322.
13. Irving, p. 215.
14. Liddell Hart, p. 350.
15. Ibid., p. 351.
16. Ibid., p. 352.
17. Irving, p. 227.
18. Ibid.
19. Liddell Hart, p. 385.
20. Ibid., p. 391.
21. Irving, p. 243.
22. Ibid., p. 253.

Chapter 6

1. Liddell Hart, *Rommel Papers*, p. 430.
2. Irving, *Trail of the Fox*, p. 269.
3. Ibid., p. 276.
4. Liddell Hart, p. 445.
5. Ibid., p. 447.
6. Messenger, *Last Prussian*, p. 176.
7. Irving, p. 284.
8. Messenger, p. 177.
9. Ibid.
10. Irving, p. 289.
11. Ibid., p. 297.
12. Liddell Hart, p. 462.
13. Messenger, p. 180.
14. Liddell Hart, p. 463.
15. Irving, p. 339.
16. Messenger, p. 194.
17. Liddell Hart, p. 492.

18.   Irving, p. 380.

Chapter 7

1.   Fraser, *Knight's Cross*, p. 554.
2.   Messenger, *Last Prussian*, p. 208.

Select Bibliography

Barnett, Correlli, ed. *Hitler's Generals.* London: Weidenfeld & Nicolson, 1989.

Behrendt, Hans-Otto. *Rommel's Intelligence in the Desert Campaigns.* London: William Kimber, 1985.

Brett-Smith, Richard. *Hitler's Generals.* London: Osprey, 1976.

Burdick, Charles, and Jacobsen, Hans-Adolf, eds. *The Halder War Diary 1939–1942.* London: Greenhill Books, 1988.

Fraser, David. *Knight's Cross: A Life of Field Marshal Erwin Rommel.* London: HarperCollins, 1993.

Hamilton, Nigel. *Monty: The Making of a General 1887–1942.* London: Hamish Hamilton, 1981.

Heiber, Helmut, and Glantz, David M., eds. *Hitler and His Generals: Military Conferences, 1942–1945.* New York: Enigma Books, 2002.

Irving, David. *The Trail of the Fox: The Life of Field-Marshal Erwin Rommel.* London: Weidenfeld & Nicolson, 1977.

Liddell Hart, B. H., ed. *The Rommel Papers.* London: Hamlyn,1984. Paperback.

Macksey, Kenneth. *Guderian, Panzer General.* London: Macdonald & Jane's, 1975.

Mellenthin, F. W. *Panzer Battles.* Norman: University of Oklahoma, 1956.

Messenger, Charles. *The Last Prussian: A Biography of Field Marshal Gerd von Rundstedt, 1875–1953.* London: Brassey's, 1991.

———. *The Unknown Alamein.* Shepperton, U.K.: Ian Allan, 1982.

Rolf, David. *The Bloody Road to Tunis: Destruction of the Axis Forces in North Africa, November 1942–May 1943.* London: Greenhill Books; Mechanicsburg, Pa.: Stackpole, 2001.

Rommel, Erwin. *Infantry Attacks.* Barton-under-Needwood, U.K.: Wren's Park
   Publishing, 2002.
Schmidt, Heinz Werner. *With Rommel in the Desert.* London: Harrap, 1951.
Strawson, John. *The Battle for North Africa.* New York: Scribner, 1969.
Warner, Philip. *Auchinleck: The Lonely Soldier.* London: Buchan & Enright,
   1981.

Index

British Indian Army
    Brigades
        21st Indian Infantry Brigade,
        96
        29th Indian Infantry Brigade,
        96
    Divisions
        4th Indian Division, 73, 76, 86
        5th Indian Division, 101–102,
        107
British Mediterranean Fleet, 102
British Somaliland, 61
Brittany, 163–164
Brooke, Sir Alan, 109
Buerat Line, 135–136
Burgdorf, Wilhelm, 176

Capuzzo, 72–73, 76
Caucasus, 88, 113
Cavallero, Ugo, 76, 87, 89, 98, 106,
    124, 128–139
Cherbourg, 170–171
Churchill, Winston, 63, 68, 75, 97,
    109, 153
Clark, Mark, 156
Communists/Communism, 23–26,
    156
Crüwell, Ludwig, 77–80, 91, 94
Cunningham, Sir Alan, 79
Cyrenaica, 61, 63–65, 67, 82,
    85–89, 129–131
Czechoslovakia, 185

"the dash to the Wire," 79, 182
de Gaulle, Charles, 187
Denmark, 160, 162–163
Der Sturmer, 39
Dollmann, Friedrich, 163, 164, 167,
    172, 173

Egypt, 61–62, 70, 72, 79, 88, 98,
    117–118, 131

Eisenhower, Dwight D., 156
El Adem, 92, 96
El Agheila, 64–65
El Duda, 80–81

Fellers, Bonner, 85–86
Fortune, Victor, 55
France, 5, 7, 23, 30–34, 37–56,
    59–61, 64, 66, 163—169,
    175–181, 186
French Army
    Armies
        Ninth Army, 46
    Corps
        French IX Corps, 140
    Free French Brigade, 93–95
    Freikorps, 23–24
French Resistance, 168, 170
Fuqa, 107, 122, 127

Gabr Saleh, 77
Gafsa, 139–141
Gariboldi, Italo, 62–63, 66
Gause, Alfred, 74, 75, 79, 80, 95,
    109, 150–152, 166
German/Germany
    became a dictatorship, 26
    and economic recovery, 25
    invasions, 7, 29, 40, 42, 59, 74,
        98
    military code, 30
    nonaggression pact with Poland,
        31–32
    see also Hitler, Adolf; Rommel,
        Erwin
German Army
    Armies
        Fifteenth Army, 162–164, 167,
            170
        Fifth Army, 6–7
        Fifth Panzer Army, 131–133,
            137, 140, 142–143

5th Panzer Regiment, 67–69, 76
8th Panzer Regiment, 141
25th Panzer Regiment, 44–45, 52–53
31st Panzer Regiment, 42
6th Rifle Regiment, 49
7th Rifle Regiment, 43–44, 53
Goebbels, Joseph, 39, 57, 59, 110, 117–118, 152, 174
Göring, Hermann, 133, 134, 148, 151
Gort, Viscount, 49
Graziani, Rodolfo, 62
Greece, 61, 63, 70–71, 151
Guderian, Heinz, 41, 48, 110
Gulf War, 136, 164–165, 182, 184–185
Guzzoni, Alfredo, 62

Halder, Franz, 74
Halfaya Pass, 70, 72–74, 78, 82
Hart, Basil Liddell, 149, 178
Hindenburg, Paul von, 25
Hitler, Adolf
  appointed chancellor, 26
  and Case Red, 51
  disobedience to, 117, 125–127
  is furious over withdrawal in Africa, 123–124, 133
  gives Rommel two options, 176
  and relationship with his generals, 34–35
  and relationship with Rommel, 3, 4, 27, 28, 52, 88, 117, 120, 123–125, 127, 132, 150, 161, 176
  tries to apply Russian experience to Africa, 125–126
  see also names of individual countries
Hitler Youth, 28, 29, 169, 170, 174

Hofacker, Cäsar von, 173, 176
Hoth, Hermann, 41–43, 46–49, 51, 53, 59
Hube, Hans, 151

Infantry Attacks (Rommel), 28
Inter-Allied Military Control Commission, 24
Invasion of Poland, 32–34, 37, 185–186
Invasion of Russia, 71, 74
Iraq war, 136, 168
Iron Cross awards, 8, 10, 51
Italian Army, 82, 104–108, 115, 117–118, 120–121, 123, 125–126, 129–136, 139–140, 142, 150–157, 183–184
  Armies
    First Army, 139, 142, 147, 149
    Tenth Army, 61
  Corps
    X Corps, 91, 94, 105, 125
    XX Corps, 75, 81, 97, 101, 114–115, 184
    XX Motorized Corps, 92
    XXI Corps, 91, 97
  Divisions
    Ariete Division, 63, 68–69, 75–76, 78, 91, 93–94, 103, 123
    Brescia Division, 68, 99–100, 144
    Littorio Division, 123
    Pavia Division, 99–100
    Pistoia Infantry Division, 108
    Trento Division, 68
    Trieste Division, 75, 91, 93–95
Italian Campaign, 150–151
Italy, 2, 25, 60–61, 85–88
  as a fragile Axis Power, 61–62, 133, 149–159, 186